THE MEDICAL CASEBOOK
OF ADOLF HITLER

Hitler's personal physician Dr. Theo Morrell *(National Archives)*

The Medical Casebook of Adolf Hitler

His Illnesses, Doctors and Drugs

by
LEONARD L. <u>HESTON</u>, MD
Professor of Psychiatry, University of Minnesota
and
RENATE HESTON, RN

with an introduction by
ALBERT SPEER

STEIN AND DAY/*Publishers*/New York

First published in the United States of America in 1980
Copyright © 1979 by Leonard L. and Renate Heston
Introduction copyright © 1979 by Albert Speer
All rights reserved.
Printed in the United States of America
Stein and Day/*Publishers*/Scarborough House
Briarcliff Manor, N.Y. 10510

Library of Congress Cataloging in Publication Data
Heston, Leonard L
 The medical casebook of Adolf Hitler.

 Bibliography: p. 172
 Includes index.
 1. Hitler, Adolf, 1889-1945. 2. Heads of state—Germany—Health
and hygiene. I. Heston, Renate, 1936- joint author. II. Title.
[DNLM: WZ313 H675H]
DD247.H5 1980 943.086'092'4 79-6031
ISBN 0-8128-2718-X

TO OUR CHILDREN

. . . it is an unhappy business that God has given to the sons of men to be busy with. I have seen everything that is done under the sun and behold, all is vanity and a striving after wind.

ECCLESIASTES i. 13–14

Contents

Illustrations
Frontispiece (facing title page)
Adolf Hitler and Dr. Theo Morrell (following page 83)
Hitler's Electrocardiogram charts (pages 152-155)

Introduction

by

ALBERT SPEER

Translated by
Richard and Clara Winston

We go too far when we no longer
know where we are heading.
Goethe, *Maxims and Reflections*

Professor Leonard L. Heston, together with his wife Renate, has here persuasively demonstrated that the characterological changes Adolf Hitler underwent during the last years of his rule were most probably due to the oral intake and injections of amphetamines. Hitler's mistrust, hyperactivity, loquacity, agitation, loss of emotional control, capriciousness and irritability seem to have been the consequence of such treatment. To the experienced medical practitioner such symptoms, to which may be added rigidity of mental processes and an excessive attachment to detail, add up to a clear clinical picture.

According to the Hestons, it is a virtual certainty that Hitler began suffering from a fateful chronic amphetamine poisoning from the end of the summer of 1942 on. But the probability exists that Hitler was already taking these dangerous drugs as early as 1936.

Only eight years after Hitler's suicide, in 1953, I drew up an account several hundred pages long of my observations of Hitler and my experiences with him as his close associate. The sections dealing with the changes in his character read like an anticipatory corroboration of the results of the Hestons' researches. Nothing so much as my own descriptions from that period convinced me that

11

Professor Heston and his wife have come to the correct conclusion.

The quotations that follow are extracts from those 1953 notes,*

'Up to 1938 Hitler had allowed his associates to take full responsibility for their assigned fields; after they reported to him he would come to an agreement with them on the general line. "Agreement" is the right word, for I recall from this early period that after long conferences he would often remark, with a sign of relief, that he had at last brought his associates around to his view. Later a crucial change took place. More and more he avoided discussion and resorted to decisions made on the strength of his position. This tendency to make his own decisions was in turn connected with his growing suspiciousness. Distrust made him a cynic, and by the end of the war his cynicism had expanded to the point of utter contempt for the German people for having failed.'

'It was striking to observe how rigid Hitler had become (from the summer of 1942 on), and how little inclined he was to grasp ideas of any moment. His mind moved along an unalterable track; he could not recover the mental agility of his earlier days. Hitler now lacked the capacity for thinking out large scale conceptions; with a kind of dull obstinacy he stuck with a course once set.'

'His irritability increased (from the summer of 1942 on). In the past Hitler had had a fine sense of discrimination. He had been able to adapt his language to the people around him. Now he was unrestrained and reckless. He would lose his temper, flush deeply, and in a rapid, loud voice breaking with excitement denounce the incompetence and mendacious cowardice of the General Staff. After such an outburst Hitler would have to pace the room furiously for a long time, wordlessly snapping his fingers, until his agitation somewhat subsided. Then again he would go back to the table to sit hunched over the map, gesturing feebly, looking up out of weary eyes at the tall, silent wall of army officers, like a stranger among them. Truly, he came from a different world.'

* These remarks are unmethodically scattered through my 1953 manuscript. I have here organized them by themes; only selections from them heavily abridged, were published in my book *Inside the Third Reich* (London, Weidenfeld & Nicolson, 1970, New York: Macmillan).

'He shrank from reality. In particular he did not want to see what the bombing raids had done to German cities. In peace-time he had loved detours so that he could see life in the streets or inspect buildings in construction. Now he had himself driven by the shortest route through the areas of rubble, seemingly detached from all responsibility as he sat stonily in the car, showing no sign of emotion.'

'Thus began (still from the summer of 1942 on) a peculiar state of petrifaction and rigidity; apathetic uncertainty, agonized inde-cisiveness, an apparent inability to deal with all important prob-lems and obstinacy when faced with them; and a permanent state of caustic irritability. Formerly, he had made decisions with almost playful ease. Now he had to squeeze them out of an overburdened brain. He no longer had inner peace and was no longer self-possessed. Rather, in a state of continual inner turmoil he was always prone to impulsive decisions. On the other hand he could also postpone important decisions for months. Outwardly, he did not appear to be moody, but we were forever dependent on his changing moods.'

'He spoke with me and others in a manner that seemed imper-sonal and aloof. The days on which Hitler made decisions freshly and spontaneously as he had done in the past, or listened atten-tively to opposing arguments, were so unusual that we subse-quently called one another's attention to the fact. The banality of the subjects he discussed during the nocturnal tea-times indicated that Hitler's threshold of irritability had become extremely low. During these nocturnal conversations he often gave the impres-sion of being mentally impaired.'

'His speech became an overflowing torrent, like that of a pris-oner who betrays dangerous secrets even to his prosecutor. In his talk Hitler seemed to me to be in the grip of an obsession. After Badoglio's defection Hitler sat up until three o'clock in the morn-ing discussing the new situation. Five or six times he repeated variations of the same ideas. During those hours he talked in a kind of waking dream, his eyes expressionless, and frequently—in keeping with his artistic nature—confounding fantasy with real-ity.'

13

'The more inevitably events moved (from 1944 on) towards the final catastrophe, the more inflexible he became, the more rigidly convinced that all his decisions were the right ones. At the same time his closest associates were anxiously observing his increasing irresoluteness. He took to making his decisions in deliberate isolation. Intellectually, he had become more and more hidebound and had hardly any desire to develop new ideas.'

About 2 a.m. on 1 January 1945 I joined Hitler and his entourage who were 'gathered around Hitler drinking champagne. The alcohol had relaxed everyone but the atmosphere was still sombre. Hitler seemed to be the only one, without the stimulation of champagne (for he did not drink), who was drunk. He was in the grip of a permanent euphoria.'

Hitler had always needed stimulants. I recall that before speeches or important conferences he would take countless Cola-Dalmann tablets.* Undoubtedly they revived him and removed inhibitions. I find my notes of 1953 stating further: 'But more important was the stimulant of popular enthusiasm, tokens of which poured out upon Hitler almost daily. Wherever Hitler went before the war, whether to the theatre or to inspect a building, wherever his car stopped for a short time during those first years of his rule, the same scenes were repeated: people beside themselves with fervour. The mass exultation was not called forth by rhetoric or suggestion; Hitler's presence alone was enough. When he went to the theatre, a large part of the audience waited patiently outside his box. Police had to be called to clear the short path for him from the exit to the street, through a crowd cheering fanatically. At Obersalzberg there was a daily procession of thousands of admirers filing past his house. When he spoke at public meetings he could be certain of finding a hypnotic atmosphere of unconditional submissiveness; it was already there when he arrived, and rose to a high pitch at the beginning of his speech.'

'I was able to observe the way Hitler, after a series of strenuous days, was revived by this kind of stimulant. In the period before the war these recurrent demonstrations of his popularity had become a tonic that was part of his life. I could see that in his

* See page 87.

stiffened self-confidence afterwards. They were as essential to him as, for professionals who set their own tasks on their own responsibility, the appreciation of their colleagues and the satisfaction of the work itself. Nothing is more difficult than to continue on a given course against the general opinion, that is, without applause.'

'The circle in which he moved after the beginning of the war could not provide him with such stimulus. No matter what the individual's attitude was, here there were no longer any eyes glowing with enthusiasm. Here there were no people so carried away with excitement that they could scarcely speak. In the matter-of-fact atmosphere of Headquarters any such adulation would have seemed ridiculous.'

Later, during my imprisonment, I discovered what it means to live under enormous psychological pressure and not be surrounded by people whose appreciation and sympathy give one emotional support. That is harder to bear than the blows of destiny themselves.

In saying all this I should not wish to suggest that Hitler's addiction was made inevitable by the circumstances of his life. There are enough examples of other historical personalities who mastered similarly desperate situations by their own strength of character.

According to Professor Heston, Hitler was in the same position as an experimental animal inasmuch as he was receiving quantities of amphetamines for a prolonged period when neither the dose nor the duration of treatment had been experimentally determined. The same thought had occurred to some of Hitler's close associates—those among them who had any understanding of the matter. In my notes of 1953 I find the following comments:

'In the opinion of Morell's antagonist, Dr Brandt, Morell used the latest discoveries on his prominent patients before sufficient experience about their effects had accumulated. He was always in favour of the latest thing in the field of vitamins, hormones, sulfanilamides, etc. and injected them into his important patients in high dosages. It seemed to us that every new discovery inspired so much enthusiasm in Morell that he recklessly began injecting these drugs at once. Hitler's other physicians feared that this continuous introduction into the bloodstream of substances that would normally be produced by internal secretion could result in a dangerous slackening of the patient's own capacity to produce. On the other hand it was obvious that Hitler was being revived and sustained by these constant doses of drugs.'

The drugs Morell gave Hitler were not generally known, only hinted at. 'Morell maintained that a wide variety of vitamins and hormones were mixed in his injections. But when asked about the composition of his mysterious mixtures, he would regularly reply: "A mixture specially compounded for the Führer."'

'A racing crew can become overtrained from overstrain. An over-trained racing shell crew, for example, becomes dull, irrit-able, and loses all flexibility. But once the rowers are past the point at which they feel they have to give up, they row on and on mechanically. This is how we viewed Hitler's situation. Hitler's entourage urged him to relieve this state of over-work by taking a longish vacation since he gave himself no opportunity to relax, not even for a few days every two or three weeks. But Morell boasted that he could keep Hitler up to the mark by his injections, without need for a vacation. Perhaps he succeeded—' so I wrote twenty-five years ago— 'in bringing Hitler just over that hump at which another individual would be driven by over-work to take a lengthy rest for fear of collapsing from natural psychic and physical exhaustion. But surely it could only be physiologically harmful to cheat nature in this way.'

'To all our remonstrances Hitler would comment: "It's easy to advise me to take a vacation. But I cannot put off making current military decisions even for twenty-four hours." Here, Hitler was the prisoner of his own system; instead of exercising leadership, he lost himself in the smallest details. Thus Hitler by far over-strained—' as we thought at the time— 'his mental capacity by his excessively strong will.' I am now convinced, as a consequence of Professor Heston's work, that this syndrome, along with others, was produced by the amphetamines he was being given.

From my 1953 notes it is evident that Hitler's close associates could only proceed by guesswork when they discussed Morell's treatments and the medicines he used. Even Hitler's personal physicians, Dr Brandt, Dr Hasselbach and Dr Hase, considered Morell's medical procedures unscientific, but they were groping in the dark. That is one more example of the potentialities for secrecy, even within Hitler's immediate entourage.

It is true, however, that 'Brandt occasionally expressed the suspicion that the injections administered to Hitler contained a stimulant in addition to the vitamins and glucose. He spoke of morphine.'*

'In October 1944, Brandt thought he was on the right track—' though in fact this speculation led him astray. 'He attributed all of Hitler's symptoms of fatigue and rigidity to strychnine poisoning.' Heston has described the circumstances in detail. Here I can supplement this story with a note of mine. 'Brandt promptly communicated his suspicion of strychnine poisoning to Göring, who scarcely reacted until Brandt asked him to read over an extract from a medical lexicon on the symptoms of such poisoning. After the reading—I was told this by Brandt—Göring was completely convinced. 'What it says here agrees precisely with what is wrong with Hitler,' Göring said. He had a copy made and took it to Hitler at once. But the only result was that Brandt was immediately relieved of his post because he had intrigued against the incomparable Morell.'

The Hestons' remarkable evidence took me by surprise because at the time no one dared to regard Hitler as an addict of any kind. Of course, Hitler himself was more than delighted to be receiving these drugs, whose pernicious effects the Hestons have so carefully investigated. 'He frequently declared: "What luck that I met Morell! If I hadn't I would have been dead long ago. He has saved my life. Wonderful, the way he has helped me." From 1942 on Hitler repeated in endless variations: "It would be an inconceivable tragedy if anything should happen to Morell. I could no longer live without him." When Mussolini visited Hitler at his headquarters shortly after the attempted assassination of 20 July 1944, Morell was summoned just before the Duce arrived. Morell gave Hitler one of his injections, and that evening Hitler was

* Morphine was used as a generic term for any addiction.

fulsome in his praise: "Again it was wonderful the way Morell has helped me. I was completely exhausted and after his injection I felt fresh again. If it hadn't been for him!" '

The question naturally arises whether Morell's treatments significantly changed Hitler's aims and the course of events. The following description applies to the Hitler I knew before and after he met Morell: 'Hitler was always inscrutable and insincere. He was always cruel, unjust, unapproachable, cold, intemperate, self-pitying; but at the same time he was the exact opposite of all that. He could be a solicitous paterfamilias, a forbearing superior, amiable, self-controlled, proud, and enthusiastically responsive to beauty and grandeur. Presumably, he like Robespierre, never truly loved anyone but himself. Obstinacy paired with skill at dissimulation, a compelling need to deceive others, had always been his traits. What Napoleon once said about Robespierre could also be applied to Hitler: "He was a fanatic, a monster, but incorruptible!" '

The psychiatrist, Ernst Kretschmer, in his *Geniale Menschen* ('People of Genius'), has examined several of Robespierre's character traits which coincide remarkably with my own picture of Hitler: Robespierre was choleric, cold and unfeeling, while at the same time he was possessed of a strong vein of sentimentality. He was extraordinarily reserved, morbidly touchy, basically disliked intimacies, and in private life was undemanding and docile. Like Hitler, Robespierre displayed a pedantic nature in which arrogance was linked with a stilted, digressive, schoolmasterly manner.'

'There was always a feeling of unreality about Hitler,' I wrote in 1953. It seems to me that he was all the more prey to his passion for power and violence because he had no deep human emotions to oppose it. So bound up was Hitler with the nihilistic element within himself that ultimately he had to destroy himself—with or without amphetamines. Even before Morell began treating him, 'all his endeavours were from the beginning limitless and irrational. That holds true for architecture; it holds true for the war, which was planned long in advance, and likewise for the economic programme, the dictatorship, and finally the annihilation of human beings. Goethe in 1799 wrote of Schiller's *Wallenstein:* "In the case of Wallenstein we have a fantastic life founded upon an extraordinary individual and favoured by an extrordinary moment in time." Those words make me think of Hitler. Goethe again, in *Poetry and Truth,* spoke of those demonic people who "emanate an uncanny force. They possess an uncanny power over all creatures." '

Hitler had already made some of his monstrous, evil errors, such as the creation of concentration camps, the persecution of the Jews, or the struggle against the Church, before he came under the sway of amphetamines. Similarly, as early as 30 June 1934 he had ordered the murders of many of his closest friends and associates of many years, as well as of opposition politicians. What sort of disruptive energy was in the man, which almost always found its outlet in sheer destructiveness?

I wrote in 1953; 'After the war many of Hitler's former associates attempted to exculpate him by establishing the theory that Hitler changed in 1938. They attribute the change to his deteriorated health resulting from Morell's treatment.' To me, on the contrary, it seems that Hitler's plans and aims never changed.

It would be a mistake to try to show Hitler as the unfortunate victim of addiction. My own view would rather be that exercising unrestricted power in the long run is bound to have intolerable effects upon the ruler. Power itself was the main drug underlying his activity. At an early stage the repeated applause of his entourage, the enthusiasm of the masses, had a toxic effect upon Hitler. He had become addicted to power, fame, untrammelled dominion and only when those indispensable stimulants began to fail would he have attempted to replace them by the effects of amphetamines. I certainly would not want to see anyone excusing Hitler on the grounds of health: 'You see, he was a sick man; otherwise everything might have turned out well.'

'Undoubtedly he had had fixed notions for years about his "race to victory". That race turned into running amok only when he began having doubts about his health.'* It may be that

* This 'running amok' began at the end of November 1937 with the plans for the dismissal of Foreign Minister von Neurath, War Minister von Blomberg and Chief of the Army Command General von Fritsch, who had warned Hitler against moving towards war. They were replaced by the pliable Ribbentrop and Keitel, with Hitler personally assuming the duties of the war minister.

19

amphetamine injections induced the recklessness which led him to run amok faster and faster until he attained his frightful goal. Back in 1953 I thought without having any inkling of possible connections with drugs, that 'in historical terms things would not have turned out better had Hitler managed to shake off the numb obstinacy that had seized him, had he recovered his ability to develop great concepts. Who can say what we were spared because Hitler remained rigid? Had he been able to make an imaginative effort to escape from the existing situation, the result would have been renewed collaboration with the enemy in the East. Many small remarks he made and many small attempts pointed in this direction. He hated the western world until the very end of his life.' In this he ran counter to the general opinion of the German people, who voted with their feet when millions of Germans fled westward from the Soviets.

Field Marshal Milch told me that during the last year of the war Professor Kalk, the well-known specialist in internal medicine, was at work on a book about the influence of severe illness upon the personalities of great historical figures. He began with Caesar. At the time we were sure that Hitler, too, would provide an interesting case for this book. Now, through the Hestons' work, Hitler's case history has for the first time become the scientific object of a medical study. I myself would not support the view that these findings in any way serve to excuse any of Hitler's acts. There is indeed a disclosure of the abnormal in the Hestons' revelations, but this abnormality is inseparable from the demonic aspects of Hitler's nature.

'We go too far when we no longer know where we are heading.' Hitler, in his romantic irrationality, never *knew* how his conceptions of 1925 could be achieved—those conceptions that were crystallized in a gigantic arch of triumph. That drawing he made in 1925 was to serve as the symbol of his plans to rule the world. He went farther and farther along this path, which inevitably led into mists and was beset by pitfalls and dark abysses. He denied all the perceptions of his intellect; he did not want to know where his road would take him, but it could only lead him to his own destruction.

Albert Speer
24 December 1978, Heidelberg

Authors' Introduction

While Dictator of Germany, Adolf Hitler had major illnesses of three organ systems: gastrointestinal, nervous, and vascular. That he was seriously ill is obvious from published descriptions of him but little attention has been paid to either the nature of the illnesses or their likely historical significance. One reason for this neglect has been sheer lack of evidence sufficient to warrant serious medical analysis of the complex diagnostic problems. We believe we have found the needed evidence. Our search began with published descriptions of Hitler and archival records. Recently declassified material from the National Archives in Washington, DC was especially helpful. By putting together information, we developed medical hypotheses testable by asking specific questions of persons who had known Hitler or had opportunities to observe him.

We found that the men and women who had known Hitler were a special group. Some were not easy to locate and some were at first reluctant to talk to us, and they had understandable reasons. Many had spent years in Russian prisoner-of-war camps. They had been hounded, misquoted and sometimes vilified by writers and journalists bent on exploiting Hitler. To some degree, most had been pictured as accomplices of Hitler. In 1975, when we began our field work, they were in their later years of life and had lost patience with inquisitive meddlers and were apprehensive about further involvement. Yet, we found them friendly and co-operative once we understood their situation and they understood that we were after hard medical data rather than gossip. They varied in their aptitude for observing and remembering medically relevant facts, but we found that specific factual questions pricked interest and memory. For example, Hitler suffered from headaches, but we had found no medically adequate descriptions of them. So we asked, 'Where in the head was the pain located? Was it throbbing? Or constant? Sharp or dull? At which times was it most intense? What made it better? Worse?' and so on until a reasonable consensus was reached among respondents and the data were sufficient for diagnosis. (The headache was due to sinus infections as will be seen in Chapter Three.) Doctors have long known that such medical questioning not only gets needed data, it also has the additional benefit of establishing a working rapport, and this we found between ourselves and those we interviewed. We felt free to return with further questions, and have done so. The evidence we found filled critical gaps.

Lack of factual evidence has not been the only barrier to a medical study of Hitler. He has been too often explained away as a creature endowed with inhuman powers and inhuman motivations—as a demon—and in the emotional climate of the post-war decades that seemed explanation enough. Frequently, the quasi-medical and over-abstract terminology fashionable in mid-century psychiatry was used to paint the demonic picture. That emotional bias will have to be put aside. It is time to stop regarding Hitler as something beyond comprehension, for he was surely one of the most important men ever to live. His actions brought military catastrophe to Germany and unprecedented emotional revulsion against a man and the output of his life. Reactions to him have decisively shaped the geopolitics and social philosophies with which we live today. Thus it is most important that from at least mid-1942 until his suicide in April 1945 Hitler was intermittently incapacitated by organic brain disease with known signs, symptoms, and predictable effects on behaviour.

Our interest in Hitler began with recreational reading about World War II. We combine the skills and training of a psychiatrist with a neurological bent, to whom the ambiguous accounts of Hitler's medical signs and symptoms posed an entertaining diagnostic puzzle that soon became a hobby, and a psychiatric nurse who was born in Germany and educated in both Germany and the US—we found that the combination of

22

medical training, specialization in psychiatry, and facility in German language (especially the ability to read medical notes in German script) was perfectly suited to the task and probably essential to it. Both of us were children when Hitler died: our attitudes towards him and his movement were (and remain) the conventional ones of rejection and revulsion. However, medical analysis must be based on the closest possible approximation to scientific objectivity. We were trained to maintain objectivity and that is how we proceeded.

This book is organized much as a medical 'work-up' on a hospital chart. Medicine has evolved standard methods for handling data that ensure accuracy and completeness at perhaps some small expense to dramatic emphasis. We will present all of the medical evidence concerning Hitler now known to us. We have worked at turning out a balanced presentation of that evidence without under- or over-emphasis of any parts and at making the whole intelligible to a non-medical audience. Also, we describe our search for evidence so that others will know where we found dead ends and where further data may yet be found. We will make diagnoses that we think are so highly probable that in the light of that evidence, few will contend them. These diagnoses imply profound effects on behaviour and we suggest medical guidelines for social, military, and political historians to use in their future assessments of Hitler and his era. Percy Schramm, a German historian who knew Hitler well, ended his biography of Hitler by assigning to medicine that responsibility for further exploration of 'the Hitler problem', saying that historians could do no more until the medical data were gathered and analyzed.[1] Now, if our objective in this book has been attained, the problem is back in the hands of historians.

We are most grateful to many persons who gave us critical help with specific technical problems. Parts of the manuscript or original data or both were reviewed by Drs Irving Gottesman, John Harris, Alan Heston, Stanley Lorens, Dale Lowther, David Lykken, Paul Meehl, Richard Meisch, Roy Pickens, Paul Winchell, Diana Tanabe, Leonard Wilson, and Neil Yorkston. Formal presentations of the data were made to medical audiences at the

23

Universities of Iowa, Kansas, Minnesota, and Southern Illinois, the Iowa Psychiatric Society and the St Paul Academy of Neurology and Psychiatry. The subsequent questions and lively discussion focused immense clinical experience and technical expertise on Hitler's illnesses.

We are also indebted to many people who smoothed our way during the gathering of data. George Wagner guided us through the massive holdings of the US National Archives. P. H. Reed of the Imperial War Museum, London, and Dr Stürzbecher, Senator for Gesundheit and Umweltschutz, Berlin, were also most helpful. Drs E. G. Schenck, H. D. Röhrs and H. Fikentscher, all German physicians interested in Hitler's medical problems, gave freely of advice and practical help. Günter and Axel Pätzold arranged accommodation and helped in many other ways to make possible efficient and pleasurable field trips in Germany and Austria.

Dr William Hausman, Head of the Department of Psychiatry, the University of Minnesota, gave us constant encouragement and administrative support and the Minnesota Medical Foundation provided partial funding which was most welcome. Finally, Dr Mary A. Puff made many helpful editorial suggestions.

HITLER: A Medical Chronology

Date	Age	Medical Event	Public Event
20 April 1889	—	Adolf Hitler born	
Sept 1905	16	Leaves school	
Winter 1905	16	Pulmonary illness	
1 Aug 1914	25		World War I begins
16 Aug 1914	25	Enlists in infantry	
29 Oct 1914	25	First combat	
5 Oct 1916	27	Wounded left thigh, evacuated	
March 1917	27	Returns to front	
4 Aug 1918	29	Iron Cross, First Class	
13 Oct 1918	29	Poison gas, blinded	
11 Nov 1918	29		World War I ends
27 Nov 1918	29	Discharged from hospital	
9 Nov 1923	36	Left shoulder injury	
14 Sept 1930	41		Nazi candidates get 19% of national vote
1931	42	Eva Braun becomes mistress	
17 Sept 1931	42	Geli Raubel suicide. Hitler depressed	
25 Feb 1932	42	Becomes German citizen	
31 July 1932	43		37.3% of national vote. Nazi Party gets plurality
30 Jan 1933	43		Hitler Chancellor
1933	43	Abdominal pain begins (at latest)	
19 Oct 1933	44		Germany leaves League of Nations, 92% of national vote endorses action
1935	45	Vocal cord polyp removed	
1936	46	Morell becomes physician	
7 Mar 1936	46		Germany reoccupies Rheinland
July 1936	47		Spanish Civil War
1937	48	Himmler—'signs of neurosyphilis'. Hitler's possible use of stimulants	
13 Mar 1938	48		Takeover of Austria

Date	Age	Medical Event	Public Event
Spring 1938	49	Narcotics for abdominal pain. Probable use of stimulants	
29 Sept 1938	49		Munich Conference agreement
15 Mar 1939	49		Hacha episode
1 Sept 1939	50		World War II begins
22 June 1940	51		France surrenders
22 June 1941	52		Attack on Russia
14 July 1941	52	First electro-cardiogram	
Aug 1941	52	Febrile illness	
Dec 1941	52	Febrile illness	
11 Dec 1941	52		Declares war on USA
Winter 1941–2	52	Likely signs of amphetamine toxicity	Winter war—Russian counter-attacks trom Moscow
Aug 1942	53	Probable amphetamine toxicity, tremor	
Nov 1942	53		Russian counter-attack at Stalingrad: El Alamein
Feb–Apr 1943	53	Severe depression	
11 May 1943	54	Electrocardiogram	
July 1943	54		Hamburg terror air raids 40,000–60,000 killed. Mussolini resigns
June 1944	55	Confused syntax	Invasion of Normandy. Rome falls to Allies. First flying bomb attacks on London
20 July 1944	55	Ruptured eardrums, bruises, abrasions, minor burns	Assassination attempt
July 1944	55	Tremor greatly improved. Ear infection develops	
Aug 1944	55	Severe depression	Allies take Paris
24 Sept 1944	55	Two electrocardiograms	
27 Sept 1944	55	Jaundice discovered	
2 Oct 1944	55	Jaundice cleared. Mentally clear	
9 Oct 1944	55	Doctors' quarrel	
22 Nov 1944	55	Vocal cord polyp removed	
Dec 1944	55	Relatively well	Ardennes (Bulge) offensive

Date	Age	Medical Event	Public Event
Jan 1945	55		Warsaw taken by Russians. Russians reach Oder river
Feb 1945	55	Stroke(s)	
Feb 14 or 15	55	Confused	
Feb–Mar 1945	55	Depressed	
2 Mar 1945	55	Loehlein eye exam	
21 April 1945	56	Nervous, fatigued. Morell leaves	
22 April 1945	56	Realized situation hopeless	
30 April 1945 3.30 p.m.	56	Suicide by gunshot. Body burned	
5 May 1945	—	Body disinterred by Russians	
8 May 1945	—	Autopsy	Unconditional surrender signed

27

First Illness

Starting in the early 1930s, Adolf Hitler began experiencing episodes of sharp, cramping pain in his right upper abdomen. The pain appeared shortly after meals, and when it did, Hitler would usually leave the room. Sometimes he returned 'after the spasm had passed', as Albert Speer described it, and sometimes he did not return at all. 'After every meal the pain begins!' Hitler exclaimed in exasperation.[1] Occasionally the pain began during a meal, and Hitler, obviously greatly distressed, would leave the table.[2] He also complained of abdominal distension accompanied by duller pain and frequent belching.[3] From the start, the cramping pain appeared for no evident reason and then disappeared after a time. There were days marked by incapacitating pain, days with only nagging soreness, and intervals of weeks to months without pain. But the pain always returned, and it was to do so for the rest of his life. He was in his early forties at the time and he had never before been seriously ill.

Physicians are often rightly accused of neglecting the reactions of their patients to their illnesses. But Adolf Hitler would have never permitted that and, in fact, his reactions to his illness tell so much about him and the sources of his later troubles that they command close attention. As Hitler's distress became evident, Dr Karl Brandt, a young surgeon who travelled with him in case of surgical emergencies, urged him in 1935 to have a complete medical examination. Brandt's suggestion was strongly seconded by Hitler's immediate circle of friends and associates, but Hitler refused, saying that he could not be seen to be ill. This was a critical decision and Hitler had understandable reasons for making it as he did. First, he was just assuming power and was consolidating his dictatorship in the face of formidable opposition. In fact, he could ill afford even hints of physical incapacity. Moreover, Hitler had developed definite ideas about how a national leader should appear and he had characteristically set out vigorously to create in the popular mind that impression of himself: strength of will, invulnerability, spartan self-denial. He was forthcoming enough about his quirks and infirmities among his immediate circle of friends and associates, but his public appearances were carefully staged by Hitler himself down to the finest details, so as to establish and maintain the impression he sought.[4] He hid his private life from public view. A medical examination, even in a military hospital as was suggested, was sure to attract unwanted attention and belly-aches did not fit his image.

Though Hitler the public man would not be seen as ill, Hitler the private man had pain and wanted something done about it. He did seek relief, but another set of attitudes profoundly influenced the results he obtained. One of his most pervasive traits was scepticism towards traditional authority, including medical authority. Helped by a prodigious memory, Hitler had educated himself through voracious reading and had picked up amounts of technical information that astounded those around him. Of course, he would consult technical experts—but they had to be prepared for sharp, precise questions, and if Hitler were not satisfied with the answers, he disregarded their advice.

And so it was with medicine. One of his doctors quotes Hitler as saying, 'He saw to it that he was regularly informed about the progress being made [in medicine] and solicited literature on it.'[5] He tended to sympathize with reform doctors who had broken away from standard practices and used 'naturalistic' treatments with herbs or massage or general conditioning measures. But he was not irrationally stubborn. In 1936, he developed a hoarse, weak voice and Dr von Eicken, a noted otolaryngologist, was called. Von Eicken found a small polyp (a benign tumour) on a vocal cord which he proposed to remove. Von Eicken described Hitler as questioning and distrustful: he accused von Eicken of hiding the full truth about his condition. But von Eicken persisted, reassured Hitler, and in a minor operation done in Hitler's quarters, the growth was removed without problems.[6] Highly intelligent, sceptical patients are familiar to every doctor and generally are dealt with readily just as von Eicken dealt with Hitler. But unhappily, abdominal pain is not as easily diagnosed or treated as a vocal cord polyp, and a squeaky voice is more of a handicap to a politician than pain after meals. Although Hitler did ask for opinions, no one could convince him to undergo the needed examinations for his abdominal pain.[7]

What he did do about his illness was entirely in character: he treated himself. Gradually, he adopted an eccentric diet that was nearly vegetarian. Guided, no doubt, by the effects of particular foods on his pain, he eliminated rich pastries and meat and continued to eliminate foods until his basic diet was vegetables and cereal—a major change for a man who had a reputation as a lover of cakes and sweets. 'Even bread and butter gave him trouble. *Zwieback,* honey, mushrooms, curds, [and] yogurt became his standard diet.'[8] At times, even milk products were eliminated and some vegetables, especially cabbage and beans, were also troublesome. Though occasionally he lapsed and would again try the rich foods he previously had enjoyed, Hitler generally followed a very stringent diet from the middle 1930s on.

He also began to treat himself with drugs. At first these seem to have been drugs purchased without prescription, but little is known about them except that there were several kinds. Hitler's chauffeur packed a valise full of these medications for use on auto trips.[9] Probably, he was experimenting to gain maximum relief, and the outcome was that he settled on one main pharmaceutical remedy for abdominal distress, Dr Koester's Antigas Pills. Dr Koester's pills were medically innocuous, as will be seen, but later, in the heat of war, they were to cause an ironic and tragic dispute.

The abdominal pain had two other main consequences. First, Hitler had suspected, apparently for a number of years, and sometimes seemed to believe, that he would have a short life. In a letter written by Hitler in 1928, he mentioned that he was then thirty-nine years old and that at best he would have only twenty more years.[10] The pain helped convince him. In 1937, he told

Albert Speer that he must accelerate his plans. 'I shall not live much longer. I always counted on having time to realize my plans. I must carry out my aims as long as I can hold up, for my health is growing worse all the time.'[11] At the same time, Hitler believed himself absolutely essential to the realization of his political and historical plans. 'By and large everything depends on me, my continued existence, my political knowledge and abilities.'[12] In this and similar assertions that he made repeatedly, Hitler was referring to the emotional hold he had on Germans, partly through accident, partly due to his unique abilities, but always as just an aspect of political reality. He had the power to achieve his dreams for Germany, but his time was limited.

And finally, his illness brought together Hitler and Dr Theo Morell, who would become Hitler's personal physician, his *Leibarzt,* from 1936 until ten days before Hitler's suicide.

Theo Morell, born 22 July 1886, was forty-nine years old when he first met Hitler. Fat, balding, and eccentric in dress, he was physically most unattractive. He elicited extreme reactions. Most of Hitler's entourage heartily disliked him, but a few defended him vigorously. His career had been unusual and undistinguished. After a short stint as a school teacher, he entered the Munich Medical School and, after graduating in 1912, worked first as a ship's doctor and then briefly as an army physician during World War I. After the war he established a specialty practice in dermatology and venereal disease located on the most fashionable street in Berlin. He also treated 'sexual neurasthenia' (mainly impotence) with various forms of electrical stimulation. Most of his patients came from the artistic and theatrical communities with a sprinkling of night-club entertainers, politicians, and bureaucrats. He was notably successful.[13]

Quite a lot can be said about Morell's medical practice. In the United States National Archives, there are thirteen rolls of microfilm containing his business and medical records. The original documents were removed from Germany by American military authorities after the war and later returned. The main period covered by the records is 1939–45, but many of the patients had been coming to Morell for several years and they probably provide a fair sample of his practice. The most striking overall impression is that Morell avoided sick people. In fact, anyone who seemed ill was referred elsewhere. Accordingly, his practice consisted mainly of persons with vague, probably psychophysiological complaints, a few weight-reduction problems, and occasionally venereal disease.

The treatments varied little. They were first of all innocuous, for Morell did not prescribe dangerous drugs and he did no surgery. In the entire set of records, we did not find a single case where narcotic drugs were used. Even barbiturates were used rarely, and then in doses too low to be effective. In contrast, he was willing to experiment with new medications, especially tissue extracts of one sort or another which he described as 'natural' treatments. For example, obesity was treated mainly with Hypophysan, a crude extract of the hormone-regulating centre of the brain. Venereal disease was treated by standard methods, though very cautiously, with respect to dosage of drugs and intervals between treatments. But the basic treatment received by nearly all of Morell's patients was Mutaflor, a preparation of living bacteria cultured from the faeces of a 'Bulgarian peasant of the most vigorous stock'. (See Appendix C.) During the preceding decades, the types of bacteria that colonized the large bowel of man had been identified and classified. The theory behind Mutaflor was that abnormal strains of bacteria sometimes displaced normal ones and produced gastrointestinal symptoms. The bacteria in Mutaflor were supposed to overgrow the pathological types and restore normal balance. The diagnosis that abnormal bacteria were present was made by Professor Alfred Nissle, a noted bacteriologist who had published original research on colonic bacteria in the early 1920s. Samples of stool were sent to Dr Nissle and reports were returned. Invariably, pathological bacteria were found and Mutaflor, Nissle's own product, was prescribed. Even after treatment the reports were nearly always still positive for pathological strains and more Mutaflor was prescribed. At the time the treatment was considered cultish nonsense by most medical authorities, though it did have a few vigorous advocates. Morell based virtually his entire practice on it.[14]

Of course, there are others like Morell practising medicine or one of the other healing arts the world over. They fill an ecological niche by providing succour for many persons for whom the main stream of medicine has little to offer. Successful practitioners of Morell's sort generally avoid doing anything that might possibly be physically harmful or specially painful, and from this it follows that much of what they do is medically useless. Some are guilty of grossly exaggerating the seriousness of an illness in order that expectations won't be too high and remission, if it occurs, will seem a minor miracle. Morell was one such practitioner. For example, there is a record of a man told by Morell that he had bacterial endocarditis, a disease invariably fatal in those days. The patient was treated by 'natural means' and was cured. A letter from him makes clear that he became a devotee of Morell.[15]

Yet Morell cannot be dismissed as a rather foolish villain. Later, isolated in endless Russia, he will be seen rising above his past and indeed, in his records, another side of him sometimes appears. Morell was not ignorant of good medicine and he was not unfeeling; some letters to patients are extraordinarily sensitive and contain sound medical advice—generally advice on how to accommodate a disability and against medical intervention—but not the letters of a quack. Rather it seems that Morell was one of those known in the profession as a 'therapeutic nihilist', one who has little regard for the efficacy of medical treatment and a fatalistic faith in the essentially inexorable natural course of disease. In the early decades of this century that attitude was certainly understandable and it is not unknown today. But why, then, did Morell stay in medicine? He doubtless believed that he was doing some good, but there was also a baser motive: simple greed. Morell was remorselessly acquisitive, as will later be illustrated. He was also keenly aware of the importance of one's social station. Letters to subordinates and juniors were peremptory and pompously condescending, even for the social milieu of the time, while he fawned on social superiors. So Morell found his niche—treating the rich and powerful for minor ailments—and he developed a large and lucrative practice. The Morells of medicine, whether quacks or nihilists, have one critical attribute: they can sell themselves and their treatments. Their success depends on engendering faith.

One of Morell's patients was Heinrich Hoffmann, Hitler's photographer. Besides being highly regarded as a photographer, Hoffmann was humorous, abreast of the latest social gossip, and a *bon vivant* who thoroughly enjoyed life. He was a charter member of Hitler's inner circle. Hoffmann believed that Morell had cured his gonorrhoea, and he esteemed him highly for this. (In fact, from Hoffmann's account of his illness, gonorrhoea was a most unlikely diagnosis.[16]) Hoffmann played a critical role in Hitler's life. He introduced Hitler to Eva Braun, who became Hitler's mistress, and later, a few hours before their joint suicide, his wife. In 1936, worried about his friend's health, he recommended Morell and brought him to Hitler.

When Morell first examined Hitler, he had probably not practised serious medicine for twenty years. He recorded that Hitler had 'difficulty with his diet' and a 'gastrointestinal upset'. He discovered enlargement of the left lobe of the liver (upper right central abdomen), swelling in the pyloric region (approximately the central abdomen), and eczema on the shins. (See Appendix A.) Professor Nissle found pathological colonic bacteria and Morell prescribed Mutaflor: Day 1, a yellow capsule; day 2 to 4, one red capsule daily; then two red capsules daily. Hitler took capsules containing bacteria cultured from the faeces of a Bulgarian peasant until 1943.[17] Hitler, for his part, was delighted. 'Nobody has ever before told me so clearly and precisely what is wrong with me. His method of cure is so logical that I have the greatest confidence in him. I shall follow his prescription to the letter.'[18] Morell and Hitler had found each other.

For some time, probably several months, Hitler felt better. There is mention of renewed trouble in late 1937, but that was apparently short-lived. Hitler was undeniably better, and he remained well until 1938. The improvement should not be surprising, for Hitler had one of those chronic conditions that wax and wane in intensity. Treatments given when a remission is

35

occurring seem to produce cures and that trick of nature has been deceiving doctors and patients since antiquity. When Hitler's pain did return, Morell turned to other drugs: first another useless nostrum, but then potent and effective treatments of the symptoms. These drugs will be discussed in Chapter Five, but they had no effect on the underlying disease process which progressed inexorably.

Subsequent episodes of illness almost certainly were related to the original abdominal pains. In August of 1941, Hitler developed a febrile illness with shivering chills, vomiting, and greatly increased cramping abdominal pain.[19] A less severe episode of the same kind occurred in December of 1941. Morell described the illness as 'grippe-like' (intestinal flu), but later, when he needed an explanation for Hitler's subsequent deterioration, he seems to have considered at least the August episode as encephalitis, an inflammation involving brain tissue. That diagnosis is most unlikely if only because the time needed to undergo such an illness and convalesce from it was not available. During the August illness, Hitler was seen frequently by visitors. Their descriptions are inconsistent with encephalitis. The longest gap in Hitler's recorded conversations is ten days, 3–12 December 1941, and there is no evidence in the conversation on the 2nd or the 13th of illness pending or completed.[20] Also, there is testimony that Hitler was never incapacitated because of illness for more than two or three days at one stretch until September of 1944.[21] Thus, the 1941 illnessses must have been short, though dramatic, and most likely gastrointestinal.

The next major episode came to attention on 27 September 1944. Hitler was strolling in the sun outside his headquarters bunker when he was seen to be jaundiced.[22] His skin and the sclera (the white) of his eyes were definitely yellowish. Jaundice, a cardinal sign in medicine, indicates severe disease, usually of the liver or the gall bladder and its ducts. Morell did not believe the evidence at first, but when he was convinced, he advised bed rest and Hitler must have agreed. For the next five or possibly seven days, Hitler disappeared from view and little is known about this period except that the cramping pain was worse than usual.[23] The jaundice cleared within a week at the most, and though the cramping pain reappeared intermittently, there was no further progression of the gastrointestinal illness during the few months remaining to Hitler. But meanwhile, from the historical viewpoint, Hitler had for at least two years suffered from a much more significant illness.

CHAPTER TWO

Neuropsychiatric Illness

Hitler's second major illness was neuropsychiatric in nature. It began insidiously and, as is usual with chronic disorders, to fix an exact date of onset would not be possible. There are hints of trouble as early as the autumn of 1937. By the winter of 1941, there were probable signs. But those early suggestions of illness are recognizable as such only in retrospect. It was not until the autumn of 1942, as the disorder was becoming definitely established, that the first unequivocal signs emerged.

In that summer of 1942, German military fortunes had reached their highest point. From the North Cape of Norway to the Pyrenees mountains and the Aegean islands, Europe was controlled by German troops. Rommel was at El Alamein and it seemed possible, even likely, that the Suez Canal would fall to him, driving the Allies from the Mediterranean. Immense areas of Russia were occupied and although the offensive against Moscow the previous autumn had failed, Russia had sustained such losses that her chances of maintaining effective resistance seemed nil. German armies were conducting two giant offensives in southern Russia aimed at the oil of the Caucasus mountain region and the great port on the Volga River, Stalingrad. All was going well although the Russian armies were retreating in good order, avoiding decisive battle. Hitler, now personally directing the war, was in his military headquarters located near the city of Vinnitsa in the Ukraine. There each morning a conference was held attended by Hitler, the Wehrmacht command, liaison officers from the other military branches, and representatives of essential civilian ministers. Reports were received, the situation was reviewed, and the highest military and state decisions were made.

On 21 October 1942, at the morning conference, there came a

first unequivocal sign of disorder. A report was received telling that a few German soldiers had climbed Mount Elbrus, the highest peak in the Caucasus mountains, and there had planted the German war flag. Hearing this, Hitler exploded with rage. Albert Speer, the Minister of Armaments and War Production, described the scene: 'Seldom did his anger erupt from him as it did when this report came. For hours he raged as if his entire plan of campaign had been destroyed by this bit of sport.'[1] The others present agreed with Speer: the climbing of the mountain was understandable horseplay of no importance whatsoever. Hitler's reaction seemed grossly disproportionate to the situation in both duration and emotional intensity. That is medically notable, and more was to come.

On the same day, there was a major quarrel with Colonel-General Halder, the Chief of Staff of the armed forces. For weeks Halder and Hitler had been debating the conduct of the campaign, sometimes heatedly, but within rational bounds. Halder regarded the two offensives as too much for German resources to sustain. Hitler thought otherwise. Then, that afternoon, in the context of that debate, Halder's aide reported an intelligence estimate that the Russians were producing 1,200 tanks monthly. The estimate was more pessimistic than usual, but such data were daily fare in headquarters to be disputed or accepted or ignored. But this time Hitler reacted furiously. He advanced on Halder and the aide who had provided Halder with the figures, fists clenched, raging: 'Don't ever utter such idiotic nonsense again. I forbid it.'[2] And again, two weeks later, General Alfred Jodl defended a subordinate commander against Hitler's charge that he was advancing too slowly. Hitler's reaction stunned Jodl: 'Never in my life did I experience such an outburst of rage from any human being.' Jodl described Hitler's rages as 'irrascible agitations . . . making unpredictable what he did and decided'.[3]

Speer, Halder, and Jodl, all three long-time associates of Hitler, were describing an apparent change in an aspect of Hitler's personality. To be sure, Hitler had always made his feelings known and he had had temper outbursts. He is described as one of those persons who react quickly and intensely, but then as quickly subside.[4] Observers had found his anger warranted in the context of the situations confronting him and, moreover, he had been so capable of hiding or controlling anger when expedient that Speer regarded self-control as one of Hitler's major assets through the pre-war period.[5] But now, the grossly excessive amount of time and emotional intensity expended on trivial events was not understandable to others. Hitler was exhibiting a significant pathological sign, morbid anger. And there also were overt acts that marked a change. After the quarrel with Jodl, Hitler left the officers' mess where he took his meals in relatively convivial company, and he never returned. Whereas he had seemed to enjoy soldierly comradeship, a tendency towards isolation became evident. He also ordered teams of stenographers to record every word uttered in the military conferences. His secure working relationships that had been gradually eroding for months were now replaced by suspicion and mistrust.

Personality change is one of the most subtle and difficult signs of illness to assess. Taken alone, morbid anger means little because it is not a specific sign of a particular disorder; rather, it is seen in several disorders and its significance depends on what occurs to other dimensions of personality. A pattern is needed and therefore we will systematically examine Hitler's intellectual, emotional and neurological functions after first completing a description of Hitler's morbid anger and its consequences.

Hitler's rage continued to erupt with increasing frequency through the rest of his life. In December 1942, General Walter Schellenberg recorded: 'Without even ascertaining the facts Hitler flew into a terrible rage . . . for three hours he shouted . . .'[6] Field Marshal Keitel described Hitler's irritability as 'unbearable'.[7] Hoffmann recorded: 'He spoke with savage contempt and anger in his voice . . . never had I heard him speak in such a manner. Never had I seen such wild, hate-filled eyes.'[8] General Heinz Guderian described Hitler '. . . cheeks flushed with rage, with raised fists he stood before me, beside himself with fury and altogether out of control.'[9]

Among many more examples that could be cited, one given by Otto Dietrich contains all of the medically important elements and can serve as a prototype. Dietrich, Hitler's press chief and a member of the inner circle from 1931 until he was fired by Hitler a month before Hitler's death, described this scene. A famous singer in German opera had died and the newspapers had not featured the story. Because there were no banner headlines as he had expected, Hitler erupted in a '. . . frenzy of rage against the press. His fury lasted for hours and made him literally incapable of work for the rest of the day.' Here again was seen the disproportionate time and intensity of his rage. Dietrich illustrated another important feature of the rages, their intermittency.

> It is hard to imagine a greater contrast in one and the same person than that between the frenzied and splenetic Hitler and the Hitler whose pleasant and likable traits [were uppermost] . . . He would appear as a deeply sympathetic, artistically sensitive being . . . People who had known him only in the second phase could not possibly imagine what the other Hitler was like.[10]

The great contrast described by Dietrich warrants emphasis. While it is true that Hitler became more and more irritable through the war years—observers are unanimous on that point—the deterioration was periodic and uneven.[11] The frequency and duration of his rages increased, but there are also many recorded instances of rationality and restraint in the face of calamitous news and even direct personal provocation. Indeed, these affective swings magnified the destructive effect of the rages. At one time composed and logical, at another raging and usually without any discernible external cause for the difference, Hitler confronted his associates with unpredictability that they could not understand and with which they could hardly cope. Heinz Assmann, a naval attaché at headquarters from 1943 to the end, described the effect:

> Those workers in close association with Hitler were constantly torn between admiration, recognition, despair, disappointment, and hatred. It was often that one felt like hating him; yet,

one would be disarmed again on the very next day by his creative ideas, his staunch confidence in victory, his amazing knowledge and his kindness.[12]

With the rages came a related change commonly seen in association with pathological anger—impulsiveness. Like most of us, and certainly like most politicians, Hitler had previously kept his options open as long as possible. In fact, he was noted more for delay in routine administration than for decisiveness, although when required he could make quick and sure decisions. What he did was to use whatever time was available to him to think through his problem, to allow it to ripen as he said, before taking action which was effective, rational behaviour until displaced by uncontrolled anger. But then Hitler became '. . . easily aroused to anger and his decisions were unpredictable, often irrational', as Guderian described him in 1943.[13] Quickly those in contact with him learned when and when not to bring up contentious questions, and more and more they learned to modify and temper his decisions. For example, in December of 1943, Hitler, in a rage, instructed Heinrich Himmler, the SS chief, to kill all prisoners out of hand. Himmler, who did not obey the order, remarked that Hitler's order was the product 'of a sick mind' and that Hitler had given 'peculiar' orders for a long time.[14] Martin Bormann, Hitler's secretary and the man responsible for transmitting his orders, often modified Hitler's decisions to further his own personal ends. As Hitler lost control of himself he began to lose control over his dictatorship. But moderation developed slowly: Hitler's immense power enforced '. . . his snap decisions with their frequently horrible inhuman consequences.'[15] This outcome was made more likely because Hitler's impulsiveness interacted in a cruelly ironic way with another of his attitudes towards leadership. He believed that any appearance of indecisiveness weakened authority; hence, he was extremely reluctant to change any decision once it had been announced. Of course, decisions were reviewed and some were changed, but getting that done was difficult at best, and the heat of pathological anger often forced tragic decision in cold steel.

Another major change in mental status was the development of pathological thinking. Two basic abnormalities of thought are recognized in pathology: a disturbance in (1) the progression (or form) of thought—the logical process—or (2) in the content of thought—what is thought about. Hitler had disorders of both.

One major manifestation of Hitler's disturbed progression of thought was becoming absorbed in detail. In military conferences, he began to neglect major strategic questions and to focus instead on minute details, often the positions of single divisions or artillery batteries. Field Marshal von Rundstedt described the change: 'Whenever formerly the general staff would present their plans there were intelligent counter questions.' Later, 'Hitler would lose himself in details, would question why this or that pillbox had not been fortified.'[16] As he was the supreme commander, Hitler's obsession with detail had grave consequences for the command structure and its operational efficiency. Every order had to have Hitler's approval. Von Rundstedt gave this bitter summary: 'The only troops I could move without permission were the sentries outside my door.'[17] And Speer noted, 'Whereas in the past he had known how to let others work for him, he now assumed more and more responsibility for details.'[18] For Hitler this was a major change. He previously had loathed details and had insisted on concentrating his time on broad issues. For example, on becoming Chancellor, he had at first attempted to wade through masses of written material piled on his desk each morning, but after a few days, he refused to look at thick documents and ordered that anything presented to him must be written on one sheet of paper.

A related manifestation of disordered thinking was mental rigidity, i.e., repetitive, stereotyped thinking, a tendency to stick too long on a few topics, to repeat too often the same ideas or phrases, to attempt to fit problems to a few formulated solutions. This is illustrated in minutes of military conferences where repetitiveness is especially notable. Often the purpose of meetings was lost because Hitler would single out some particular point and stick to it tenaciously. A small number of abstract phrases came to be used as answers to concrete questions that came up, such as,

43

'no retreat; only with permission; accepting the risk; concentrated bold and determined attack; fanatical will'. Over and over again the same few responses to entirely different situations.[19] In social conversations, too, Hitler became repetitive and lost in detail. 'His conversations became monologues, endless repetitions of the same ideas.'[20] 'He became intellectually more sluggish and showed little inclination to develop new ideas. It was as if he were running along an unalterable track . . .'[21] His social conversations came to be dreaded by his entourage who had to sit with him far into the night listening to the same stories over and over again.

Again, the pathological signs vacillated in intensity. Sometimes a more moderate defect in progression of thought was evident: distractibility. Hitler became overly attentive to incidental environmental factors as is often seen in hyper-alert states. Keitel described the effect:

> As Hitler could never keep to the point on these occasions but diverged on still further problems as they were introduced by other parties, the midday war conference lasted an average of three hours . . . although the strategic and tactical questions should not as a rule have consumed more than a fraction of that time.[22]

At another extreme, there were occasions when Hitler's thinking became disorganized, but those must have been quite rare because only two instances have been recorded. Speer describes one such episode. On 26 June 1944 Hitler addressed a group of about one hundred representatives of the armaments industry. He fumbled for words, became distracted in mid-sentence, neglected transitions, and was obviously confused.[23] The problem was not slurred speech, as commonly occurs in intoxicated states; rather, it was Hitler's confused syntax and organization.[24] This is a notable incident in an orator of Hitler's skill and experience. Dr Erwin Giesing described another such incident which occurred in February 1945.[25] Again, the evident problem was confusion.

44

Finally, sometimes Hitler's thinking was relatively clear and flexible. In the 26 July 1943 military conference, Hitler quite rationally discussed various options for retreat. A speech to his military commanders after the loss of the Battle of the Bulge in December of 1944 was utterly realistic, logical, and effective. The varying intensity of pathological signs was an essential feature of his disorder.

One salient abnormality of content of thought was increased suspiciousness. He became chronically suspicious and behaved accordingly, as is profusely illustrated in accounts of the period: 'He lied assuming others lied to him,' said Guderian.[26] Gradually, Hitler became preoccupied with his suspicion and mistrust, and, as that happened, a trait emerged which is regularly associated with pathological suspicion, a tendency to project blame on to others. He 'put the blame for his own mistakes on others . . . a character trait that became more and more prominent from the winter of 1941 on', said Dietrich.[27] Suspiciousness, as much as anger or faulty progression of thought, undermined Hitler's human relationships, especially with his military commanders.

One remaining variable in Hitler's mental status became pathologically affected, mood. Mood can be briefly defined as the prevailing emotional tone—usually described with words such as 'happy' or 'sad'. We sometimes feel mildly depressed or happy without apparent reason. Superimposed on that foundation are reactions to events, such as an unfavourable event which would elicit depression, or good fortune which would make for happy feelings. So it was with Hitler until that same autumn of 1942. Then his mood became dissociated from his previously normal basal state and came to have an inconsistent and distorted relationship to events. The prevailing change was towards over-elation: Adolf Hitler became chronically 'high', or, in technical language, hypomanic. But there also were at least three episodes of depression, and while the elevation of mood was clearly pathological, the depressions at first appeared as relatively normal reactions to events. However, the depressions, too, probably were pathological.

45

It is easy to underestimate the contribution of mood to daily life and hence, how much distortion of reality can be caused by swings of mood. Mood colours every single facet of life. When an individual is depressed, his past, his present, his future; everything he has done; all that he owns; all of his human relationships; all that has happened and all that will ever happen becomes darkly tinged to utterly black, depending on the depth of the depression. When on the manic side, everything good seems possible, problems dissolve, the past, present and future seem vividly important and cause for elation. The environment is assessed and dealt with against this background leading to grave errors in judgement. Thus, depression causes overestimation of obstacles and paralysis of action, while mania leads to over-optimistic neglect of real hazards and problems.

Broadly, Hitler's sequence of mood swings began with over-elation through the last four to five months of 1942. Then, during the latter part of January of 1943 to March, Hitler was depressed. The depression followed the immense German military disaster at Stalingrad, so there was apparent good reason for it. Morell announced publicly that Hitler was suffering from manic-depressive illness, advised a three-month rest, and began treatments for depression.[28] This period is notable for its lack of descriptions of Hitler, because he withdrew and became less active, as is common in depression. Then in the spring of 1943 another shift in mood occurred. After early 1943, according to Speer, Hitler never again seemed depressed. Rather, Speer explains, he was always optimistic, often unreasonably so in view of the desperate course of events. 'The more inexorably events moved towards catastrophe, the more inflexible he became, the more rigidly convinced that everything he decided on was right.'[29] Heinz Linge, Hitler's valet, also described Hitler to us as usually highly optimistic, even elated, despite reality that was increasingly grim, and he seemed to become more impervious to disastrous news from the spring of 1943 onward. However, Linge also remembers depressed episodes, and he is supported by evidence. There were periods of depression that Speer, who saw Hitler only every two or three weeks on average, probably missed, and one episode that he may have not recognized. In late August 1944, Hitler is described as having lost all interest and is quoted as 'welcoming the end of life with release from worry, sleepless nights, and great nervous suffering. It is only a fraction of a second and then one is freed from everything and has one's quiet and eternal peace.'[30] In March of 1945, Speer describes Hitler as having tears in his eyes and goes on to say that this was frequent in those days.[31] Those are typical signs of depression. There is nothing to indicate that depressions after the spring of 1943 lasted more than a week or two. They were surely mild and short and the prevailing mood was over-optimistic as Speer, Linge, and others describe it. Hitler was pathologically elated from at least the autumn of 1942 onward, except for depression through early 1943 and briefer depressions in August of 1944 and February of 1945. Depression also may have been associated with his suicide in April of 1945, as will be seen.

One trait frequently seen with elevated mood is grandiosity, but assessing that feature in someone like Hitler is not an easy task. To the lay observer Hitler may seem to have always been overly optimistic and grandiose. As a boy who had failed in school, he planned the rebuilding of his home town. He wrote of his plans for the conquest of Russia while he was in jail. While Hitler did retain perspective, and probably did not consider those plans as certain of accomplishment as would be the case if he had been pathologically grandiose, he clearly took them more seriously than most of us take our daydreams. But we would be wrong if we thought of such plans as evidence of psychopathology, because Hitler, in those earlier times, had planned and acted realistically so as to accomplish his plans—and came terribly close. However, from 1942 on, his plans and optimism no longer had a plausible ring, even for a man with the most extraordinary abilities. And his grandiosity became confounded with his rigid thinking. For example, in a conference on 20 December 1943, clearly optimistic and expansionistic in mood, Hitler interrupted a military situation report to ask about the production of flame throwers and then ordered production to be trebled. Through the rest of the meeting he fixed on flame throwers, saying that they were the certain answer to the impending Allied invasion of Western Europe.[32]

The tone of his remarks then and on many other occasions carries little suggestion of analytic thought: they were grossly unrealistic and over-optimistic. There are a whole succession of such unreasoned expectations: the Tiger tank, rushed prematurely into battle by Hitler, was to reverse the retreat in Russia; the rocket weapons would defeat England; Roosevelt's death (in April of 1945) would somehow give him the victory; the Stalingrad army could be supplied from the air; a successful counterattack in Hungary in 1945 would lead to rebellion in Russia. Schramm gives a good example with details.[33] Hitler planned the Ardennes or 'Bulge' offensive of December 1944, starting just after the assassination attempt of 20 July 1944. The concept was sound and Hitler worked out the operation in all of its detail. Yet, there was no possibility of success. If the offensive gained its objective, which was Antwerp in Belgium, two flanks of known length would have to be defended. There were thirty-two divisions available—obviously deficient manpower. German staffs and Hitler had had plenty of experience with such operations, but Hitler simply refused to accept the arithmetic showing that what he proposed was impossible. Objections were brushed aside by grossly over-optimistic assertions. Schramm then contrasts Hitler's planning in 1944 with that of 1940. In 1940 Hitler confronted analogous problems, but then he dealt with them realistically and devised ingenious and militarily sound ways of overcoming or bypassing them. That could be said of Hitler on very few occasions afterward.

In delineating patterns of disorder, functions that remain normal are as important to note as those that become impaired. The most important normal finding is that Hitler had no impairment of memory, especially memory for recent events. Hitler was always noted for his prodigious memory, and he continued to astound observers right up to the end. To be sure, he occasionally remarked in exasperation that he had forgotten something or other, but those were clearly social expressions and medically meaningless. There also are occasional comments in voluminous literature describing Hitler that suggest loss of memory, but taken in context, the episodes described can be as well explained by failure of concentration. On the other hand, there is overwhelming testimony that his retention was unimpaired. As described, he planned the Bulge offensive of December of 1944 in all of its details. That feat would be incompatible with significant impairment of memory. Field Marshal Albert Kesselring described Hitler on 8 March 1945 as having an 'astonishing grasp of detail'.[34] Transcripts of military conferences during the last period depict Hitler as often lost in detail but in full command of those details. Keitel described Hitler as absolutely lucid up to 29 April 1945. The next day he committed suicide by gunshot.

A less important negative finding is that Hitler most likely did not experience delusions or hallucinations. Some persons who have written about Hitler describe him as delusional, but their use of the term is literary, not medical. A delusion is a fixed, uncorrectable false belief. Hitler did hold false beliefs from time to time as everyone does, but they were not held long enough to be considered fixed or uncorrectable. Towards the end, he did speak of mythical new armies, which would reverse the tide of battle; but other conversations show with pitiful clarity that he was quite aware that no troops were available to fill out the divisions that existed on paper. Moreover, even such transient false beliefs would have to be attributed to his over-optimism and grandiosity and thus would be secondary to his altered mood. This is an important technical distinction. There is no good reason to suspect delusions or hallucinations of any kind, although it would not be surprising if he did in fact experience one or the other or both.

Through the same period that he developed the abnormalities of mental status we have described, Hitler's neurological functions began to decline, pathologically. The first sign was a tremor involving Hitler's entire left arm. Tremor is a most important neurological sign and there are several varieties and several causes. In its earliest stages, Hitler's tremor has been described as rhythmical oscillation of the fingers of the left hand, with enough motion at the elbow and shoulder to cause visible movement

49

beneath the uniform jacket. We had practised the various types of tremor, and we demonstrated them for persons who had known Hitler. The tremor that was recognized by all was a rhythmical and very short to and fro excursion of the fingers and wrist at our maximum rate of oscillation (about six beats per second) which was strong enough to cause the whole arm to move. This is the tremor known in neurology as an exaggerated physiological tremor, or action tremor. The tremor tended to worsen whenever Hitler attempted purposive movement with his left hand. Hence, it was not a resting tremor, one that lessens with purpose movement, and it may have been an intention tremor, one that grows worse with purposive movement. One cannot be absolutely sure because Hitler had learned little tricks to minimize the tremor when his arm was at rest: for example, keeping his thumb and forefinger pressed tightly together or holding his arm tightly against his waist, but when he moved the arm he lost such controls. Also, Hitler was strongly right-handed so there was little opportunity to observe purposive movement of his left hand. The tremor did get worse with emotional arousal '. . . a barometer of his excitement', said Speer,[35], and the tremor's intensity was used as a danger signal by those around Hitler. The tremor, like the mental signs, waxed and waned over the next years and, overall, there was the same trend towards worsening. During the early spring of 1943, the tremor spread to involve the left leg, at first occasionally, later almost constantly. Hitler learned to control the leg tremor by wrapping his foot behind the leg of a chair and pressing forward.[36]

The next stages in his neurological decline were disturbances in locomotion. About February of 1945, Hitler's gait became slowed and shuffled, and he seemed to drag his left leg. We also demonstrated abnormal gaits for persons who had known Hitler. The one recognized as closest to Hitler's was this: a normal though short swing and step of the right leg and foot then the dragging of the left foot up to the right by rotating the pelvis forward, with the left toe, staying in contact with the floor. We did not succeed in precisely duplicating Hitler's gait in the opinion of our observers because our minimal effort seemed to exaggerate Hitler's actual disability. However, the qualitative effect was definitely recognized. The weakness of the left leg appears not to have been apparent to observers for more than a few weeks but the slowness persisted. Guderian described Hitler's gait as '*schleppend*', translatable approximately as 'slow-motion—as if carrying a heavy burden'.[37] Never again is Hitler described as moving about normally. He developed a stooped posture, and appeared weak, sick, and old.

Dietrich records that 'Hitler's doctor'—he must have meant Morell—said that Hitler had had a slight stroke in early 1945.[38] The focal weakness of the left leg and the subsequent slowing is consistent with that conclusion and so is a sign recorded by Morell who noted an 'increased left patellar reflex' (see Appendix A—this is the 'knee jerk' reflex which often is increased on the side of the body affected by brain injury). But much of the evidence also is consistent with another sort of pathology, muscular rigidity. In some neuromuscular disorders, muscle tone is increased so that movements are slowed and stiffened. Parkinson's disease features that sort of rigidity and that diagnosis has been suggested several times to explain Hitler's ills.[39]

The distinction between rigidity and weakness is an important one to make, and the most direct evidence appears in newsreel footage. Newsreels showing Hitler were surely edited to show him at his best, but because of repeated rumours that he was dead or incapacitated, he did have to be seen. One newsreel does illustrate the slowing and the impression of illness prominently mentioned by observers describing Hitler in early 1945, and is a useful marker of the extent of the disability. The film was released on 15 March 1945, but it could have been made at any time before that. Hitler, seen only from the waist up, moves very slowly up to a table in a dimly lit room, pivots to face the table and, leaning forward, firmly grasps the edge of the table with both hands and waits. Then, at Hitler's nod, an aide pushes a chair into what must be the back of his knees.[40] That Hitler did require this sort of help to sit down for a short time in late February and early March 1945 has been described in written accounts.[41] The impression from the film is of weakness, not rigidity, but one cannot be sure.

In other films, there is evidence inconsistent with rigidity of the arms and face, which are parts commonly first affected. When Hitler walked, however slowly, his arms moved in a normal swinging movement; that movement is often lost in Parkinson's disease. And in the last pictures of Hitler, made during April of 1945, definite smiles can be seen.[42] Testimony by observers generally does not support rigidity. Published accounts of the period describe Hitler with words like 'loose' or 'flabby'. Those terms are unlikely descriptions of a person suffering from muscular rigidity. Morell does not mention muscle tone. Drs Erwin Giesing and Hans-Karl von Hasselbach both had limited occasions to manipulate Hitler's arm while treating his injuries in July and August of 1944. Giesing thought later that there was very minimal rigidity. Von Hasselbach thought there was none.[43]

Probably the best evidence is that of Heinz Linge, who attended him up to the end. Linge did not help Hitler dress and did not have many opportunities to actually touch him, but he was usually close by and observed Hitler in the routines of daily life. Linge clearly remembers the slowing and weakness, although he regards most written accounts of the period as exaggerating Hitler's ills. He told us that he is quite sure there was no rigidity. The evidence is reasonably clear though not conclusive: Hitler probably suffered from weakness and not muscular rigidity.

Towards the end the tremor began to affect his right hand. During the last days he was using a rubber stamp to sign his name and the uniform of the fastidiously neat Hitler was stained with food that he could not manage to get to his mouth.

We have emphasized that the course taken by Hitler's neuropsychiatric illness was a fluctuating one, but the dates when he was relatively better or worse are difficult to specify. The times were frantic with activity and there are many obvious errors in dates in the published literature. Hitler was, of course, secretive and few persons had access to him over a long enough period of time to establish a baseline upon which to register changes. Throughout the war, Hitler divided his time between his several military headquarters and shorter periods at his Bavarian home near Berchtesgaden. In general, it appears that he was relatively clearer mentally and less irritable at Berchtesgaden. However, there were two periods in 1944 when he was notably much better, and those periods provide important diagnostic information.

The first such episode followed the assassination attempt of 20 July 1944. On that day, Hitler was in his headquarters in Rastenburg, East Prussia, where, at the daily military conference, a time bomb was exploded. Because he was partly protected by a heavy table, Hitler received only superficial injuries. Several others were killed. But there was a surprising benefit: the tremor disappeared. Hitler himself said, 'At least there was one good effect [of the bomb]. It almost cured my illness. My left leg always trembled a bit when the conferences went on too long, and it used to tremble in bed. Now all that is gone.'[44] Others agreed. The tremor did disappear, or at least greatly lessened. Just when this happened is not clear, but it was certainly within a few days after the explosion. Tremors do not usually go away, and the fact that Hitler's did is most important. But the improvement did not last. Again, the timing is uncertain, but from a few days to two weeks after the explosion, the tremor returned.

Hitler's mental state during that period is difficult to interpret. He was certainly enraged about the assassination attempt, but the anger in this case was appropriately directed from his point of view at those who had tried to kill him. Only the degree of anger seemed excessive to observers. 'What had been hardness became cruelty,' said Guderian.[45] The evidence does not allow us to judge whether the pathological anger improved or not. But Dr Erwin Giesing, an ear, nose and throat specialist who was called to treat Hitler's injuries, did describe a favourable change in Hitler's thinking. Hitler took an intense interest in his treatment, borrowed one of Giesing's textbooks and, characteristically, astounded Giesing by the range and amount of information he had assimilated. But then, about six weeks later in early September, Giesing described Hitler as 'less pleasant, flighty and rambling'.[46] The evidence is weak, but it does seem that Hitler's mental state did improve somewhat and then relapsed in a pattern similar to that followed by the tremor.

The next period of improvement was just after the period of jaundice in late September of 1944, and this time the improvement in thinking was definite. Speer saw Hitler during his convalescence and his conclusions were unequivocal. 'He was normal! Absolutely. All of the mental and intellectual decline that had worried all of us had cleared. He was clearer than I ever remember seeing him any time in the war.'[47] Speer was in charge of armaments production and frequently discussed extremely complicated matters with Hitler. He was in a position to observe Hitler's thinking closely and his assessment certainly carries special weight. However, there were others, including two physicians, who were struck by Hitler's apparent well-being.[48] The fact that Hitler's thinking did improve so dramatically is extremely important medically, as will be seen. But the improvement did not last and by mid-October descriptions of Hitler again contain all of the pathological elements.

There was one other period of at least partial remission around Christmas of 1944. On Christmas Day he is described as clear and forceful, and on 28 December he gave a clear and realistic speech to his military commanders that has been preserved.[49] He was 'as spellbinding as ever' for his guests on New Year's Eve. Minor fluctuations continued, but overall, from that time on, his course was one of rapid deterioration.

That completes the review of the salient features of Hitler's mental and neurological condition. Starting at the end of the summer of 1942 at the latest, he exhibited morbid anger, rigid thinking, and excessive attention to detail; he was sometimes easily distracted, was often pathologically suspicious, and was generally over-optimistic, sometimes to the point of pathological elation and grandiosity. He also developed a tremor involving first his left arm, then later his left leg, and finally his right arm. In early 1945, he developed a focal weakness of his left leg, and either generalized weakness or just possibly muscular rigidity that interfered with normal locomotion. All of these conditions improved from time to time, only to worsen again, and on at least two occasions in 1944 he was seen to be normal or nearly normal. His impairment disabled him intermittently and brought about a major turn in history, for Hitler had a record of intellectual innovation, flexibility, and extreme effectiveness. We will later review the medically relevant aspects of his premorbid capabilities and accomplishments. However, medical analysis best proceeds by first completing the description of all illnesses, and Hitler suffered from several other afflictions, including some that were most important to his history.

CHAPTER THREE

Other Illnesses

Sometimes doctors discover unsuspected disease in the way that Morell found Hitler's heart disease: through a little luck, some blundering, and some admirable medical practice. While the story at first will seem illogical, it will become morbidly self-evident. The parts of a medical history have a way of fitting together.

In late 1942 or early 1943 Morell began taking Hitler's electrocardiogram with unusual frequency; at least once a month, but through some periods as often as every week.[1] There appears to have been no medical reason for such a practice which at first seems meddlesome or even bizarre. But in fact in Führer Hauptquartier in the midst of history's most immense war, isolated in Russia from medical facilities and colleagues, Morell was attempting to monitor a life-threatening treatment programme. He did not know what to expect and the literature of medicine had few precedents to guide him. Forced to practise medicine, Morell was doing his best, though at the same time he was trying no doubt to safeguard himself against the consequences of disaster. What he did was take a portable electrocardiograph with him from headquarters to headquarters and he made a tracing whenever he thought one was needed. Sometimes, Hitler asked for a cardiogram himself, which suggests that he understood much about his own condition and its management.[2]

At least four of the many tracings were sent off for expert interpretation to Dr Karl Weber, a cardiologist at the Bad Nauheim Heart Institute. Those tracings and Weber's interpretation are preserved in the Morell records and can be seen in Appendix C. Recently, we had the tracings interpreted by two American cardiologists. A tracing dated 14 July 1941 was thought by Weber to show evidence of 'coronary sclerosis'—arteriosclerotic disease of the coronary arteries which supply the heart muscle with blood. The American cardiologists regarded the tracing as normal and in their opinion Weber's interpretation was due to over-reading, which was typical of that stage in the development of electrocardiography. Less than two years later, on 11 May 1943, there were definite changes that Dr Weber again interpreted as evidence of 'coronary sclerosis'. However, the American cardiologists called these changes 'non-specific S–T changes', meaning that no specific pathology could be associated with them. For example, one possible cause for the changes was the drug digitalis which Hitler may have been taking at the time (see Chapter Five). But then on 9 September 1944, two separate tracings were made and sent to Dr Weber and on those there were definite abnormalities, which while not diagnostic, were most likely due to infarction (a 'coronary' or 'heart attack'). The abnormalities might also be due to strain on the heart from high blood pressure but Hitler's pressures probably were not high enough. The changes are of indeterminate age and therefore might have developed at any time after the electrocardiogram of 11 May 1943. One clue suggests infarction shortly after June 1943. In the Morell microfilms there is an article torn from a medical journal dated June 1943 which deals with the treatment of a myocardial infarction.[3] There are few other medical articles in Morell's records and none of them deal with heart disease.

The reaction of Hitler and Morell to Hitler's heart disease contains puzzling elements. Although the modern interpretation of the electrocardiographic evidence is that Hitler had significant cardiac abnormalities of uncertain cause and prognosis, Morell and Hitler had only Weber's more pessimistic reports describing rapid progression of serious disease and grim prognosis. Because the electrocardiogram was (and is) regarded as a reliable diagnostic tool, Morell and Hitler must have credited Weber's reports. But they kept the whole matter tightly secret and that raises questions. Of course, Hitler would not have wanted his military commanders, much less foreign enemies, to know that he had a major illness which might abruptly end his life. But, as we have described, among his intimate social group he had generally been open about his physical health and his feelings about it. Morell too was talkative and headquarters personnel lived closely together for many years. Several of those we interviewed had been told by Morell about other aspects of Hitler's medical status and were sure that Morell would have told them about any serious illness. But none was told. The secret apparently had successfully been kept between two men. Even Hitler's valet, Linge, who was on friendly terms with Morell, did not know about the frequent electrocardiograms and certainly had no idea of their results. Most were scheduled when he was absent and often plans were changed when moving the apparatus would have attracted too much attention.[4] Secrecy was made easier to maintain because Hitler had no significant public signs or symptoms of heart disease. He did not complain of pain which would have suggested heart disease. No one remembers any symptoms associated with heart failure—breathlessness with exertion or rapid tiring or swelling of the ankles. The interrogation after the war of doctors who had known Hitler discovered no evidence of heart disease except that Morell himself said that Hitler once had swelling of the ankles (see Appendix A).

In summary of the evidence so far presented, we can say that Hitler probably did have significant myocardial (heart muscle) disease and may well have suffered an infarct in the late spring or early summer of 1943. However, he did not suffer any lasting physiological effect and the heart disease itself did not have significant medical effects. But Hitler and Morell knew from Weber's reports that heart disease was 'rapidly advancing' (Appendix C) and they lived with that secret knowledge from then on.

Hitler did have borderline hypertension. Morell recorded several measurements of blood pressure which ranged between 140–150 systolic and 90-100 diastolic.* Morell also noted that

---

* Blood pressure is measured in millimeters of mercury. The systolic pressure is the pressure in an artery at the time when a pulse of blood pumped by the heart reaches the point where the measurement is made. The diastolic pressure is the low reading between pulses of blood. For a man of Hitler's age, 140 systolic and 90 diastolic are considered the upper limits of normal blood pressure.

Hitler's blood pressure rose to about 170-200 systolic when he became emotionally aroused. Hitler apparently had a labile hypertension; his blood pressure was not well modulated but rather rose to significantly elevated levels at times. Although this may have contributed to Hitler's vascular pathology, he probably did not have symptoms directly attributable to hypertension.

His headaches were a different matter because Hitler was extremely distressed by them. Although they came infrequently, they tended to last several days. The pain was localized in the forehead mainly about the eyes and was increased by pressure applied to the affected areas. The pain tended to be worse at night when Hitler was lying down, and improved through the day. Those signs and symptoms are characteristic of sinus headaches attributable to inflammation of tissue lining the sinus cavities of the skull with blockage of normal drainage. Over the years, Hitler had sinus irrigations several times. There are descriptions of typical results: pussy discharge and relief of pain.[5] Unlike what has so far been described, here is at last a typical everyday affliction.

There was one bout of severe respiratory illness when Hitler was sixteen. Little is known about the episode except that the lungs were involved and convalescence was prolonged. Hitler was weak for a month or two but then slowly recovered completely. The illness has the main features of tuberculosis, but a severe viral pneumonia is also a possible explanation. Its importance for Hitler is that the episode gave him a final reason for leaving school.

We have mentioned the vocal cord polyp which was removed on 5 May 1935. In November of 1944 the same condition recurred and again a polyp was removed. These operations are not significant except that observers have attributed Hitler's high creaky voice during these periods to his general decay or 'hysteria'. Not so. He had simple uncomplicated polyps.

We turn now from medical conditions to injuries. In World War I he was wounded twice. The first was a minor wound of the left thigh, probably from shrapnel, and recovery was complete. Then on 13 October 1918, less than a month before the Armistice,

Hitler came under poison gas attack and suffered an eye injury that temporarily blinded him. He described a night of gas attacks that felled some of his comrades.[6] The next morning his eyes began to burn and his vision dimmed. For a time he could not see at all. He was evacuated to a military hospital and by the end of the war had largely recovered.

Hitler's temporary blindness has been widely regarded as hysterical, but it certainly was not. Burns and irritation of eye tissue sufficient to cause temporary blindness was a common effect of poison gas.[7]. The inflammation and swelling are there for all to see and Hitler's military record describes wounding by gas.[8] Hitler's own description of the episode, although brief, is entirely consistent with gas injury and inconsistent with hysteria.

The next injury came during the 'beer hall *putsch*' of 1923 when Hitler led a misguided and spectacularly unsuccessful attempt to seize power in the German state of Bavaria. When police gunfire ended the affair, Hitler either fell or threw himself to the street sustaining an injury to his right shoulder. From all description of the injury, there appears to have been an uncomplicated ligamental strain, or perhaps only a bruise, although Morell's records state that Hitler said he had a fracture of the glenoid process, a part of the shoulder joint.[9] How Hitler may have learned the diagnosis is unknown, but whatever the injury the shoulder was stiff for a year or two, and afterwards gave him no further trouble.

In the assassination attempt of 20 July 1944 both of Hitler's eardrums were torn by the explosion and he was thrown against a door frame, resulting in bruises and abrasions about his right elbow and right knee. His ears were treated by Dr Erwin Giesing, then with the army and the only specialist in ear disorder in the area around the headquarters. Two days after the explosion, Giesing was taken to Hitler. Hitler said, 'Doctor, I hear you are taking care of my friends [the others injured in the explosion]. I have had for the last two days a pain in the right ear, cannot hear well, and they tell me that I shout too much.'[10] Hitler also complained of dizziness and difficulty balancing on his right leg. Giesing found a large perforation of the right eardrum along with considerable blood as well as a smaller perforation of the left. He also found a partial loss of hearing, a tendency to sway to the right and nystagmus to the right. Nystagmus is a deviation of eye movement and, like the dizziness and difficulty in balancing, is to be expected with injuries of the inner ear. Giesing cleaned the ears and trimmed small granulations growing at the edges of the torn eardrums. Healing was complicated by an infection in the right ear that persisted for several weeks and for this reason Giesing continued to attend Hitler up to the time he discovered the jaundice on 27 September.

There was one other condition whose significance cannot be adequately assessed. On 2 March 1945 Hitler was seen by Dr Walter Loehlein, an ophthalmologist and Director of the Berlin University Eye Clinic. Hitler complained that for about two weeks he had been seeing through his right eye as through 'a thin veil' and that he suffered from a light stabbing pain in his eye. This was of great concern to Hitler. He had remarked to several persons that he feared that he was losing his eyesight, and those remarks have since been interpreted as hysterical. Dr Loehlein did a complete examination and some of the negative findings are significant. He found no increase in intraocular pressure (no evidence of glaucoma), normal retinal blood vessels (no evidence that Hitler's hypertension was cause for serious concern) and normal neurological reactions of the pupil (these reactions are abnormal in several neurological illnesses). What he did find in the right eye was a turbidity of the vitreous humour, the gelatinous material that fills the eyeball, a condition which Loehlein attributed to small particles, probably derived from blood cells. Loehlein thought that a small haemorrhage had occurred, caused by a 'transitory variation in [blood] pressure possibly caused by a vessel spasm' (see Appendix A). The condition was treated conservatively, with application of heat, and cleared up over the next weeks.[11]

Those are the essential elements of Hitler's medical history. Moving from description to diagnosis to analysis requires that we now look more closely at the pertinent and possibly pertinent aspects of Hitler's life history.

CHAPTER FOUR

Personal Medical History

We now turn to an examination of Adolf Hitler's origins and of his life up to the beginning of his first illness. This information would be found in a medical history in a section headed 'personal history' or 'social history' and would consist of a brief narrative description of members of the patient's family and of their social and economic circumstances. These data serve several purposes. Genetic factors predispose to many diseases including major psychiatric and neurologic disorders that might be suspected in Hitler. Advances in behaviour genetics have come very rapidly over the past few years and there are new possibilities to consider.

In this connection, overt disease in a relative of Hitler's would, of course, provide important evidence because it would increase the likelihood that Hitler would have had the same disease, but even seemingly minor physical or mental deviations in one of his relatives would be notable because they could be associated with genes capable of disastrous effects if present in Hitler. Conversely, if there is no evidence of overt disease or significant deviations among his relatives, the likelihood that Hitler suffered from a genetic disease is lessened. Of course, the family history can only alter probability estimates: an important factor but not conclusive. Hitler would not necessarily have had the same genes or the same diseases as his relative. The personal history of Hitler himself, which is also a part of this section of the work-up, will also alter probability estimates and it will be a more powerful influence because thereby some diagnoses can be excluded. Many illnesses begin within fairly discrete age intervals. If the age of risk has not been attained or has been passed without development of a particular illness, that illness is most unlikely to be present. That sort of analysis will be important in the case of Adolf Hitler.

Finally, changes in mental status as exhibited by Hitler require for evaluation a baseline of premorbid social and intellectual history.

Adolf Hitler was born on 20 April 1889. His boyhood was spent in three villages, all located in a small area of north-west Austria adjacent to Germany and Czechoslovakia. The landscape is typical of central Europe: low wooded hills, narrow valleys, and here and there, the ruin of a mediaeval castle. The effect can be softly beautiful in sunshine, or, as often, mysteriously foreboding when storm clouds are low on the hills. The Danube flows from west to east through the area which has made it for centuries a thoroughfare for peoples and armies. Generations of Adolf Hitler's ancestors were probably moulded by this geography, but despite intensive investigation by historians, most have remained anonymous. His most remarkable known relative was his father.

Starting as a shoemaker's apprentice without money, education or connections, Alois Hitler advanced to a responsible and well-paid position in the Austrian Civil Service. That move from the peasantry to secure middle class status was unusual in nineteenth-century Europe. It is a fact that Alois Hitler was an illegitimate child, but careful scholarship has discredited the story that his father (Adolf's paternal grandfather) was a Jew.[1] Like so many Hitler stories, this one is most likely untrue. The probable father of Alois was one of two brothers, Johann Nepomuk Hüttler, who later took over the rearing of Alois, or Johann Georg Hüttler, who later married Alois' mother.[2] That is notable not because of the illegitimacy of the birth, as about one-third of Austrian births in that period were illegitimate, but because Adolf Hitler's mother was a granddaughter of Johann Nepomuk and a grandniece of Johann Georg. Most likely Adolf's father and mother were related and hence, their union was inbred. This would increase the probability of recessively inherited traits in their children but otherwise would not be medically important, and neither Adolf Hitler's illnesses nor those of his siblings can be attributed to inbreeding.

Adolf's father was a stern man, strict with his children, as he was with himself. Every surviving document that he wrote has flawless spelling and grammar. This is an example of the diligence and stamina through which he achieved the highest position he could possibly attain in the civil service. His contemporaries described him on the one hand as a cheerful man who kept bees as a hobby and regularly enjoyed a few beers and evening singing in the local tavern, and on the other, as a stodgy bureaucrat. At age sixty-five, while waiting for his noon meal, he was suddenly stricken and died. The local paper, a liberal publication for the day, described him in a lengthy obituary as a man of 'progressive ideas, cheerful, with civic sense, a temperate family man'[3]: a respected community leader. Alois Hitler has been called alcoholic, but that diagnosis can be excluded because none of the criteria for it was present. Indeed there is no evidence of significant behavioural pathology of any sort and because his last illness was his only one, there is only one medical clue; sudden death in those circumstances suggests a vascular catastrophe involving the heart or brain.

Adolf Hitler described his mother, Klara, as an angel.[4] Twenty-six years younger than her husband, she was his third wife; both of her predecessors had died of natural causes after a few years of marriage. Klara Hitler was described as a quiet unpretentious woman who was a quick and neat housekeeper and a loving mother. She died age forty-five of a rapidly progressive breast cancer. The record is thin, but again, there is no evidence of behavioural pathology and no evidence of heritable medical disease likely to affect Adolf.

Six children were born to Alois and Klara Hitler of whom only two, Adolf and Paula, survived childhood. A brother and a sister died of diphtheria, another brother died of measles, and a third brother died of unknown causes a few days after birth. Many deaths, but again not remarkable for the period, and there was no evidence of genetic disease. Adolf's surviving sister, Paula, born in 1896, appears to have been intellectually dull but otherwise normal. She never married and worked as a housekeeper through her life, at times for Adolf in his Obersalzberg home. An American interrogation officer who had interviewed her after the war described her to us as a typical German housekeeper.[5] Some of her letters survived. They are coherent but do suggest limited intelligence.

Alois was an only child but Klara Hitler had two sisters, Adolf's aunts. One, Johanna, was a hunchback, but not unusual in any other respect. The cause of her deformity is unknown. Another sister, Theresa, seemed quite normal.[6]

The only definite hint of behavioural pathology appears in one child born to Alois and his second wife, Franziska Matzelsberger. (Alois' first marriage was childless.) A boy and a girl, half-siblings to Adolf, were born of that union of whom the girl, Angela, was apparently normal. But the son, Alois, left home at fourteen after a quarrel with his father. Subsequently he drifted to Ireland, England, and back to Germany, working mainly as a waiter but on the way he received two jail sentences for theft and one for bigamy. In later years, he settled down to operating small restaurants and night-clubs. A diagnosis of antisocial personality, a trait with some degree of heritability, might be considered, but the evidence is far from conclusive.[7] As Adolf's half-brother he and Adolf would, on the average, have 1/4 of their genes in common. As far as is known, that is the medical history of Adolf Hitler's family. There is no evidence of the major psychoses, schizophrenia or manic depressive illness. There was no dementing or neuromuscular illness. While all of these illnesses can reasonably be eliminated from consideration, the evidence is insufficient to eliminate lesser abnormalities. But that is often the result obtained in practice and Adolf Hitler's family would be considered quite routine in any medical history.

Adolf Hitler's early days are not known in any detail. Because of the deaths of four other children and the age of Alois, who was in his sixth decade during Adolf's infancy, Adolf may have had an unusually intense relationship with his mother. There was no evidence of feeding difficulties, temper tantrums, or childhood neurotic traits. It seems that his childhood was unremarkable.

At first school was a happy experience and Adolf received high grades through his fifth school year. He described himself as a leader in boyhood games, such as Cowboys and Indians or the British versus the Boers, and in the small towns of his boyhood his intelligence and energy probably did make him conspicuous over his peers. Then in 1903, when Adolf was thirteen, his father died. There had been for some time friction between them about choice of a career: Adolf wanted to become an artist, but his father insisted on the civil service. By this time in Realschule in Linz, a city of 50,000, Adolf rebelled against authority and school, and school teachers became the focus. A teacher looking back on the Adolf Hitler of 1904 described him as 'distinctly talented but lacking in self-discipline, obstinate, high-handed, intransigent and fiery-tempered'.[8] That year he was promoted, but only on the condition that he leave school. He transferred, apparently only because his mother insisted, to another school of about the same academic standing. But in 1905 he got low or failing marks in all subjects except physical education, and that autumn he left school permanently. For the next year, his seventeenth, Adolf did little. He was described as lanky, pallid, shy, and always fastidiously dressed. His mother had moved to Linz after the death of Alois, and there Adolf took daily walks through town, attended the theatre, read, and planned the rebuilding of the city. He had one friend, August Kubizek, who later wrote about his recollections of this period.[9] There can be no doubt that the relationship between the two boys was reciprocal and had depth. They were real adolescent friends. Adolf, according to Kubizek, was passionate, easily aroused, and full of dreams and grand plans that he would describe at length.

Hitler's failure in school must be seen in perspective. The academic pathway he entered was extremely demanding and very few even got admitted to secondary school. No doubt Adolf had the intellectual capacity to complete school, but he could not manage his stormy adolescence at the same time. Hitler himself said that he failed in school, '. . . out of spite', and 'For me, adolescence was an especially painful period'.[10] But no useful psychiatric prognoses follow from this. Adolescence is a difficult time in life but unless major legal or civil consequences result from adolescent behaviour or unless the maladjustment is prolonged and severe, the period is not a good indicator of adult outcome. However, some of Hitler's personality traits that were present during his adolescence did persist. He remained emotionally expressive and conscious of appearance. From that time onward he despised business routine and bureaucracy, and from some unknown source, despite his failure in school, he became utterly convinced of the essential rightness of his outlook and of his own capacities.

In September of 1907, Adolf Hitler, then eighteen, left Linz for Vienna, and full of confidence took the examination for entry into the Vienna Academy of Fine Arts. Of one hundred and twelve applicants taking the examination, eighty-four failed, including Hitler. Shortly afterward his mother became ill with her terminal illness and in December she died. Adolf was genuinely grief-stricken and it was two months before he again took up his life.

In February of 1908 he returned to Vienna to try again. He had an excellent letter of recommendation from his mother's landlady and there still exists a courteous reply from Hitler. At the end of February his friend Kubizek joined him in Vienna and the two young men shared an apartment until the following September. Then Hitler again was denied admission to the Academy and shortly thereafter he abruptly left Kubizek. There was no quarrel and no goodbye. Hitler simply moved out while Kubizek was away on a visit home, and left no forwarding address.

Many erroneous impressions must be corrected about the next period in Hitler's life, ages nineteen to twenty-four. Hitler later described himself as impoverished, often hungry, and others have said he lived as a tramp in a succession of flop houses. Careful scholarship has since filled in a much different picture. In fact, Hitler had an income from inheritance and an orphan's pension of 80–100 crowns monthly, or about that of a minor civil servant.[11] Moreover, he made a fairly good income through much of this period from the sale of his paintings, mainly souvenir postcards depicting Vienna scenes. Hitler painted, a succession of partners sold the works, and Hitler received half of the income. According to Maser, who has critically reviewed his painting, Hitler did have significant talent.[12]

His painting also accounts for part of the misinformation that for so long has obscured his life in Vienna. Hitler once accused one of his partners of pocketing more than his half of the proceeds. That man, who was convicted in court and served a jail sentence, later became a prime source of detrimental information used by Hitler's early biographers and political enemies. Such sources have been slowly discredited, but the impressions they have created have seriously hampered attempts to objectively assess Hitler. He did stay in a men's hostel, but not a 'flop-house' as denoted by the American term. The inhabitants of the hotel were a cross-section of single Austrian males: retired army officers, working men, minor clerks. Hitler surely saw hunger, but he suffered very little from it if at all. His later descriptions of his hunger and poverty in *Mein Kampf* appear to have been calculated to win the political sympathy of those who really had known deprivations. What Hitler actually did through the first years in Vienna was to behave as a few sons of the middle class of that day behaved and as many young people behave today. He read, painted, attended opera, passionately argued art, architecture and politics, and stayed up as late as he pleased. He stayed in Vienna until just after his twenty-fourth birthday in 1913. By that time his adolescent turmoil was behind him. He was working on a regular schedule at his painting and had established a secure social position in the men's hostel where he had come to be regarded as a resident intellectual and good comrade.[13]

Those years in Vienna are important to Hitler's medical history because during them many of the group of psychiatric afflictions known as 'personality disorders' would have become evident. None appeared. Hitler had one adverse entry on his civil record: he did not register for military conscription because, he later said, he did not respect the Austrian government. Not an unusual attitude for a German-speaking Austrian and not a sufficiently unusual act for a young male European to warrant suspicion of underlying psychopathology. One would like to know more about some aspects of his life, especially his sexual development, but the record is incomplete. At that there would have to be new evidence of some extreme deviation in a major area of adjustment such as sex to warrant reconsideration of the question of personality disorder.

In May of 1913 Hitler left Vienna for Munich, where for fifteen months he lived much as he had in Vienna. He gave as reason for the move that he wanted to obtain formal training in painting. In Munich he rented a room in a private home and his landlord and his family became his lifelong friends and political supporters. But his plans for a career were interrupted by World War I because Hitler, already a resolute if not fanatical German nationalist, eagerly enlisted in a Bavarian infantry regiment.

That he was a brave man and a genuine hero is unquestionable. He went through four years of trench warfare, was twice wounded and, in addition to several lesser medals, was awarded the Iron Cross, First Class, Germany's highest military medal and a distinction rarely achieved by an enlisted man. He was never subjected to disciplinary action and was regarded as a reliable, obedient, and very lucky soldier. From descriptions of some of his comrades it does seem that he was not a full participant in the give-and-take of camp life. No doubt he was different. However, Hitler obviously succeeded in personal relationships because several wartime comrades, including his sergeant and his captain, later worked closely with him in building the Nazi party, though both by then were his subordinates. Hitler the soldier was a highly successful person. Military service is used in psychiatric assessment as a sort of litmus test. Those with significant personality disorders are unlikely to stand up to the stress. Hitler did. His successful period of service is also strong evidence that his adolescent problems with authority had been successfully outgrown.

From the time Hitler left the army in 1920 until the early 1930s. when the abdominal pain began, there were no significant medical problems. There was only a spectacular development of a personality with few parallels in history. Neither medicine nor psychology has the tools needed to explain such a phenomenon. Hitler, not even a citizen of Germany, without money, without influential family or friends, went from discharged corporal to undisputed master of one of the two or three most powerful nations on earth. His rise cannot be explained by deception or intimidation. Hitler organized, influenced, and won over adherents; he was passionate or he was quietly rational. His popular fame came from his speeches before mass audiences, but he was also extremely effective in small groups and with individuals. Indeed he especially liked dealing 'man-to-man' as he described it, with a handshake when agreement was reached. In small groups he could be charming and jovial and he was invariably courteous to women. He was, above all, extraordinarily capable of grasping a situation and behaving so as to move events according to his own ends. Germans often use the term *Fingerspitzengefühl* to describe the Hitler of this period. It denotes an instinctively correct 'finger-tip' feeling for social situations. Hitler did have the great advantage that his goals were always clear to him; never has he been accused of muddling objectives. His rise to power was helped along by economic depression, a weak government, and a military defeat in World War I which brought with it terms from the victorious Allies that were seen in Germany as humiliating and unjust. These were exceptional times, but all times are exceptional in some respects; Hitler exploited the political environment available to him and no one can say how he would have fared in a different political environment.

Though he became effective beyond our capacity to explain, it is hard to identify new elements in Hitler's personality. He did demonstrate prodigious energy, stamina, and persistence which were not obvious in Vienna. And for a man previously noted mainly for interest in music and art and for unprecedented political ability, he demonstrated a surprising knack for technological innovation. A few examples: he promoted the national network of Autobahns; he insisted that the Volkswagen, another of his conceptions, must have an air-cooled engine to preserve mechanical simplicity and be shaped like a 'beetle', Hitler's word, to minimize wind resistance; he initiated exploration of methods for obtaining domestic gas from sewage and using wind to generate electricity. Later he was to grasp the tactical concept of massed armour and the strategic promise of the Manstein Plan for invading France, which Hitler himself may have conceived before Field Marshal von Manstein did. He virtually designed the famous '88' artillery rifle and the Tiger Tank and he equipped Stuka dive bombers with sirens to heighten their psychological effect.

The evidence forces us to conclude that when he became Führer of the Germans, Adolf Hitler had not demonstrated psychiatric impairment. He was profoundly unusual, certainly, but he was unusual in effectiveness: clarity of objectives, clarity of analysis in view of those objectives, and unprecedented ability to grasp the motives of people *en masse* or individually and enlist them in the achievement of those objectives. These conclusions differ markedly from those so far printed by scholars or propagandists alike who present Hitler as a psychiatric casualty with demonic powers. But if demonology can be dismissed, it can be confidently asserted that there is no evidence of psychiatric impairment up to the middle of the 1930s at the earliest. The evidence has been sought with meticulous care by us and by many persons very strongly motivated to find it. It has not been found and in view of Hitler's unarguable achievements it appears unlikely that it is there to be found.

We know that this conclusion will be troublesome to many because it leaves Hitler's wickedness out of the accounting. But a diagnosis, even if supportable, does not account for wickedness, and most wickedness cannot be attributed to psychiatric disorder. Hitler's antisemitism, which was well established before his assumption of power, cannot provide grounds for a psychiatric diagnosis because antisemitism was at that time extremely widespread and is more accurately described as the European norm than as a symptom. One may condemn antisemitism on ethical grounds provided by any serious moral philosophy or on logical grounds because of the grossly fallacious overgeneralization required to make the antisemitic argument. But a diagnosis or pejorative psychiatric description of Hitler, especially one unsupported by evidence, would add nothing to the evil except perhaps banality.

There were, however, three elements in Hitler's personality that presage his disastrous ending. All were small quirks that would warrant no particular psychiatric comment were it not for

71

the outcome. Only later, and greatly exaggerated, can these traits be seen undoing him.

From Kubizek, his boyhood friend, onward, those who knew Hitler remarked on his utter faith in his own convictions and his relative inaccessibility to the views of others. Through the period of his rise to power, this tendency was well compensated partly because Hitler became socially polished and partly because his convictions were concerned with overall goals, his 'granite foundation' as he put it. Hitler was highly flexible on everyday questions of tactics and even longer term ones of strategy. Perhaps Hitler's intensity of conviction was normal in the sense that it is needed by anyone seeking great political power for any purpose. Nevertheless, he was certainly less modifiable than most of us by the criticism of others or by self-examination.

Another problematic trait was manifest in the rhetorical trick of posing a series of questions that could only be answered 'yes' or 'no', thus inevitably leading to a conclusion. The effect is to exclude middle ground, to picture the world as composed of black or white alternatives, and Hitler used this device so frequently in his speeches and in his social conversation that it became a source of headquarters' humour. However, we cannot know the extent to which the fallacy intruded into his private reasoning processes. Again, during the rise to power the products of his thought showed flexibility and the ability to make fine distinctions. Any potentially fallacious processes were well compensated. Yet even in his most serious moments the tendency to either-or reasoning could be manifest; in 1936 Albert Speer overheard Hitler musing to himself: 'There are two possibilities for me, to win through with all my plans or to fail. If I win, I shall be one of the greatest men in history. If I fail, I shall be condemned, despised, and damned.'[14]

The remaining trait was his refusal to accept limitations imposed by human biology, which he attempted to evade by using drugs.

CHAPTER FIVE

Medical Treatment

A medical examination always entails inquiry into past treatments because treatments not only influence the course of an illness, they often produce their own signs and symptoms. We will therefore go systematically through those received by Hitler.

At first Hitler treated himself, and, as we have seen, settled on an eccentric, largely vegetable diet and Dr Koester's Antigas Pills. Dr Koester's pills contained extract of belladonna and extract of strychnine which would yield two drugs accounting for nearly all of the pharmacologic effect of the pills: atropine about 0·2* per tablet and strychnine, about 3·0 mg per tablet.[1] The recommended dose was two to four pills before each meal, but Hitler did not strictly observe such prescriptions and may have taken up to twenty pills daily.[2] Twenty pills would yield about 1·3 mg of atropine and 20 mg of strychnine per meal, or a maximum daily dose of about 4 mg of atrophine and 60 mg of strychnine. Atropine is usually given three to four times daily in doses of 0·5 to 1 mg. Thus, Hitler was getting enough atropine to provide him with a therapeutic dose, the main effects of which would have been to slow the contractions of the smooth muscle lining the gastrointestinal tract and decrease secretions of associated glands and secretory cells. A secondary effect must also be considered: atropine is mildly effective in relieving certain tremors. Strychnine is a central nervous system stimulant but it acts mainly below the brain at the level of the spinal cord. The drug was for decades used as a 'tonic' but it is now recognized that the supposed therapeutic effects cannot actually occur in man because the dose

---

* Drug doses are usually measured in *milligrams*—abbreviated *mg*. A mg is 1/1000 of a gram. A gram, the basic mass unit in the metric system, is about 1/3 of an ounce.

cannot be made large enough. A single dose of the order of 100 mg may produce toxicity marked by hypertonic musculature, hyper-reactivity to sensory stimuli, and finally convulsive seizures and death. Lower doses are without noticeable effects. Strychnine is very rapidly inactivated in the body and therefore cumulative increases of its concentration in tissues are thought not to occur.[3] Hitler could hardly have got a significant dose of strychnine from Dr Koester's pills—he would have had to have rapidly taken at least thirty pills at one sitting. There is no hint that he had convulsions or other signs of toxicity which would have occurred if he had reached large enough doses.

The other type of non-prescription drug used by Hitler also was physiologically innocuous, but it carried grave psychological portents. Starting some time well before the onset of the abdominal pain, Hitler began to take laxatives, inaccurately assuming that he thereby would avoid gaining weight.[4] Again he experimented before settling on Mitilax, a phenolphthalein preparation with no toxic potential. Later he used other laxatives and enemas (see Appendix C). Those who knew him agree that he was one of those persons who could easily have become portly and, ever mindful of his appearance, he battled against gaining weight. Again he was tending to his image: 'Imagine the leader of the Germans with a pot belly,' he said.[5] This early comic attempt to circumvent normal biology is ominously portentous. For Hitler was not seeking relief from pain or any symptom of illness; despite his self-proclaimed 'iron will' he was unwilling to tolerate the limits of normal physiology and he tried to escape its bounds through self-medication. Laxative abuse begins a deadly history.

Morell's first treatment with Mutaflor has been described. Gradually, over the years, Morell added more and more drugs, some used for only a short period, others used chronically. To his American interrogator, Morell gave a list of twenty-eight different drug preparations, some containing combinations of active ingredients (see Appendix C). Overall, the drugs used by Hitler ranged from innocuous to bizarre. They demonstrate Morell's willingness to experiment with new drugs, especially tissue extracts, but even judged by the standards of the day, most of the dosages used were too low to have significant pharmacologic effect.

Although Morell's treatments had little substance, Hitler's use of drugs is critically important to understanding the course of his illnesses. Moreover, there are many clues in the list of drugs to the thinking of Hitler and Morell and to the nature of the interaction between the two men. In 1938, after the failure of Mutaflor, Morell began to treat Hitler's abdominal illness with intramuscular injections starting with Glyconorm. The mixture of proteins in this preparation could have led to allergic reactions, but could not have had any beneficial effect whatsoever. At about the same time Morell also used leeches to remove blood from Hitler.[6] Although this mediaeval practice had passed out of medicine in England and America, it was still used occasionally in Germany and other nations. The next drug tried, Euflat, was not listed in any of the indices of that day. Morell's description of ingredients in Euflat does not include weights, but none would be likely to have significant effects except papaverine, a drug that became part of the next and quite effective treatment regimen.

Starting early in 1938, Morell abruptly gave up meddling and instituted potent and effective treatment of the abdominal pain using a method exactly as recommended in a quick reference text of the day.[7] That treatment became the standard one until the end. The new drug was Eukodal, a synthetic narcotic, which was combined in one syringe with Eupaverinum, a synthesized papaverine. The combination was administered intravenously. Eukodal (dihydrohydroxy codinone) is still available in Europe and is nearly identical in its chemistry and pharmacologic activity to Percodan (oxycodone hydrochloride), which is used in both America and Europe. It was first marketed as an effective analgesic that was also non-addicting. Finding such a substitute for morphine has long been a cherished dream of the pharmaceutical industry. Several times success has been widely claimed for new products as it was for Eukodal, but thus far drugs which give effective pain relief have proved to be addicting. In the case of Eukodal, the analgesia produced falls between morphine and codeine but the addictive risk, despite all hopes and initial claims,

75

proved rather closer to morphine. However, because of the claims made for it, Morell and Hitler probably thought the drug was non-addicting. Papaverine is one of the many products derived from the opium poppy, but it is not an addicting drug. Eupaverinum is a synthesized molecule identical to the one provided by nature. The standard ampoules of Eukodal contained 20 mg of active drug, and an ampoule of Eupaverinum contained 30 mg.[8] We received a description of exactly how those drugs were used.

Dr Richard Weber was a young associate of Morell's who took charge of the Berlin office while Morell was with Hitler. In the Morell microfilms, Weber is described as an occasional substitute for Morell at Führerhauptquartier. Dr Weber, who now lives in semi-retirement in a small Westphalian town, told us that he was on call to Hitler on several occasions and did in fact treat him once in October of 1944, just at the end of the period of jaundice. Morell was away overnight visiting an ill relative and Dr Weber was called late one night. The room was poorly lighted so Dr Weber cannot be sure if Hitler was still jaundiced, but he did appear to be in pain. Dr Weber had received no real medical briefing from Morell, but he had been told how to treat the abdominal pain. He mixed together one ampoule each of Eupaverinum and Eukodal and slowly injected the solution intravenously until the cramping pain was relieved, injecting as much as 20 mg of Eukodal and 30 mg of Eupaverinum.[9] This would be a standard and effective treatment for pain such as Hitler's because Eukodal would provide analgesia and both narcotics and papaverine weaken and slow the rhythmic contractions of the smooth muscle which lines the gastrointestinal tract. These contractions propel food through the stomach and intestines and the secretions of the liver and pancreas through their ducts. Slowing and weakening the contractions could be expected to relieve the pain, as in fact it did.

Morell had found an answer for the abdominal pain, but he must have been drawn into the more vigorous treatment of Hitler with mixed feelings. Before, patients who had not done well after trials of innocuous treatment were sent elsewhere. Now, with his famous and even revered patient, Morell must have known that he was far beyond his capabilities and that he had everything to lose if he failed. Why then did he continue? Certainly, one reason was that Morell was using his newly elevated status to build up a considerable pharmaceutical empire. He had taken over a manufacturing plant near Hamburg, known as Hamma, the main product of which was a vitamin preparation, Vitamultin. Large amounts of Vitamultin were distributed through government sponsored programmes to the armed forces and industrial workers. Other acquisitions of pharmaceutical manufacturing plants followed in Czechoslovakia, Romania, and Russia, and there was more government business.

Another lucrative product was Russlapuder, a totally ineffective anti-louse powder which Morell succeeded in establishing as the standard anti-louse prophylactic for German armies despite the ready availability of effective preparations. Typhus, a louse-born illness, would continue to kill thousands of German soldiers. Morell was convinced of the efficacy of Russlapuder by an experiment: lice avoided areas dusted with it and when the powder was actually poured on them, some died.[10] Morell clearly seemed to believe in his product and would certainly have not sentenced men to die of typhus. He was just incredibly greedy and scientifically naïve. The same attributes led him to say in 1944 that he had discovered a greatly improved penicillin; his product was worthless.[11] But he was becoming rich and could see that he would become still richer. All that would be threatened if he left Hitler. Also, because of his position, he was treating many of the most important men in Germany and their families: Goebbels, von Ribbentrop, and many others. One of Morell's subordinates, a Dr Georg Zachariae, treated Mussolini, and Morell consulted with Zachariae whenever Hitler and Mussolini met.[12] Finally, there was the very considerable personality of Hitler himself. Pleasing such a man must have been most rewarding psychically as well as financially, while displeasing him, even at that early stage, might have been dangerous. Step after step Morell and Hitler led each other on.

We must return to Eukodal because it was a narcotic drug to which Hitler may have become addicted. Because questions

77

about addiction will recur several times, we will first present some general background. One hallmark of addiction is tolerance. The dose of a drug producing tolerance must be increased over time in order that the effect of the drug should remain constant: in other words, one must increase the drug dose to get the same drug effect. This result depends on at least two phenomena. First, exposure to some drugs produces an increase in the body's production of the enzymes needed to degrade and inactivate the drug. Because the drug is more rapidly destroyed, more drug is needed. Secondly, the cells affected by the drug become, though incompletely understood, homeostatic mechanisms less liable to the changes in activity induced by the drug. Again, more drug is needed. These adaptations and possibly others yet unknown allow persons who regularly use certain drugs to take amounts of drug far beyond the lethal limits of those without prior exposures. Only a few drugs used in medicine produce noticeable tolerance: through 1945, those were only alcohol, narcotics, barbituarates and related sedatives, and amphetamine and related stimulants. Other drugs available then can now be shown under laboratory conditions to produce low grades of tolerance, but the effect is clinically unnoticeable or unimportant. The other main correlate of addiction is withdrawal. Abstinence from an addictive drug is associated with distress that is relieved by readministration of the drug. The addicted person is dependent on the drug to avoid withdrawal.

Whether or not Hitler was addicted to the narcotic Eukodal cannot be determined by the available evidence, but addiction is unlikely. He was certainly tolerant to the effects of one or more of the drugs Morell gave him. Several observers, including Brandt, the physician, described increasing dosages of a drug unknown to them in order to attain a constant effect, but another drug will be shown to be a more likely culprit than Eukodal.[13] Weber gave only one ampule of Eukodal to Hitler in October 1944, but Morell started using the drug in 1938 at the latest, so at the time of Weber's treatment, tolerance had obviously not developed. Finally, there is no record suggestive of withdrawal from narcotics. The main gap in the evidence is that the frequency of the injection is unknown. Although there is great individual variation, a narcotic must be used rather frequently before addiction occurs. Hitler's pain was episodic and there is no way of knowing whether or not sufficient injections were closely enough spaced to produce addiction. Actually, addiction *per se* matters little anyhow, because Hitler would not have been appreciably affected so long as he had a drug available to ward off withdrawal.

Hitler suffered from chronic insomnia, for which he used sedatives nearly every night through the war years. Barbiturate drugs, potent sedatives, were included in two preparations, Optalidon and Brom-Nervacit. Barbiturates are divided into groups according to the length of time after administration that they become pharmacologically active and the total duration of their action. The short-acting preparations (rapid onset, short duration) produce for many people highly pleasurable relief from tension and a sense of well-being. Those are characteristics of drugs liable to abuse. The longer-acting preparations produce few, if any, pleasurable effects and they are not often abused. Because the barbiturates used by Hitler were of the longer-acting kinds, there is little reason to suspect over-use or any effect other than simple sedation. The other sedative drug on the list is bromine, an ingredient in Brom-Nervacit, but the dose was quite low (see Appendix C). Over-use of bromine produces a distinctive clinical picture and Hitler had none of its elements.

Several drugs on Morell's list were aimed at Hitler's cardiovascular system. About autumn 1941, Morell started intravenous injections of the cardiac glycosides Strophanthin and Prostrophanta, which is the former with added vitamins. Strophanthin is a rapidly acting digitalis preparation, equivalent to ouabain in American medicine, and digitalis has for centuries been the standard drug for heart failure. Molecules of the drug attach to the membrane of heart muscle fibres, causing increased strength of contraction and slowing and regularization of the heart rate. In the use of digitalis we find an intricate puzzle, for there was no evident reason for giving Hitler digitalis at all, and even if there were adequate reason, Morell's administration at first appears so incompetent as to negate any possible medical

79

benefit. Morell said that he gave digitalis because of the electrocardiographic reports of Dr Karl Weber, but those reports provide no medically competent reason according to standard practice then or now. Also, Morell stated (see Appendix C), that he gave injections of '0·02 mg a day for periods of approximately 2–3 weeks' and repeated that treatment several times over the last three years of Hitler's life. However, the dosage must be incorrectly typed for the standard ampoule contained a standardized dose of 0·25 mg. Moreover, the drug was used in a way which provides ample evidence that Hitler did not actually need it.

There are two main problems for the physician prescribing digitalis. First, digitalis has no effect until the level of drug in the tissues reaches therapeutic levels. Usually a full 'loading' dose, known as 'digitalizing' dose, is given over a short period of time in order to quickly attain therapeutic levels. Then a lower 'maintenance' dose is used to keep tissue levels at that point. People vary widely in both digitalizing and maintenance doses which must be carefully adjusted for each individual. Moreover, digitalis is a toxic drug with a narrow range between a dose too low to be effective and one too high. There are rules of thumb that allow the physician to select dosages likely to be safe and effective as well as several clinical signs which allow monitoring the effect of the treatment. Strophanthin, the drug which Hitler received, is the most rapidly acting digitalis preparation, achieving peak effect in a couple of hours and then remaining effective for only half a day or so. Its modern use is, or should be, limited to emergency situations where rapid digitalization is essential. Oral digitalis preparations which are effective for much longer periods are then substituted to provide a maintenance dose. The minimum digitalizing dose of Strophanthin is 0·25 mg, and even if that amount had been sufficient for Hitler, the drug would have been effective for only a few hours. Treating someone for only three weeks also makes no sense medically: if digitalis is needed, it is nearly always needed for the remainder of one's life. Then why was Morell prescribing digitalis? Moreover, why was Hitler taking it? Hitler would have insisted on explanations and we see only one possible: digitalis was being used by Morell for the same reason he took frequent electrocardiograms. He was afraid of a cardiovascular catastrophe. Morell was giving 'Strophanthin cures' which was fairly standard practice in German medicine of the day.

Looked at in this way, the administration of digitalis makes some sense—a desperate gamble, but Morell and Hitler may have concluded that they had better use the only method available to them of possibly improving cardiac function. The choice of drug preparation also makes sense. If Morell anticipated great stress on the heart and if the stress was intermittent, he would choose a drug that was active immediately, and one that would be eliminated quickly after the stress had passed. In this context, his choice of drug was the best possible for his purposes. Ironically, digitalis has in recent years come to be used by many physicians for exactly the same reasons, for example, before a major surgery. The bumbling Morell was fighting his dubious battle fiercely and perhaps effectively.

The other drugs used for their cardiovascular effects (and likely for the same reason) were Cardiazol and Coramin. Cardiazol (or Metrazol, as it is known in the United States) is a central nervous system stimulant which, in large doses, causes convulsions. Coramin (nikethamide) also is a central nervous system stimulant very much like Cardiazol, though both drugs were thought to be primarily cardiovascular stimulants at the time Morell used them. If Morell's treatment schedule is correctly reported, these drugs were given ten drops daily for a week and were used only a few times. Ten drops of either drug would be less than half the effective therapeutic dose. Neither drug is a euphoriant; indeed, their effects are unpleasant, so excessive use would have been unlikely.

The remaining drugs on Morell's list need little comment. The hormone preparations were given to Hitler for depression during the winter of 1942–3. Morell was no doubt desperately casting about for an antidepressant treatment but, in fact, only one effective treatment for depression was known at the time, electroshock therapy, and it obviously could not be used if for no reason other than the common side-effect of loss of recently acquired memory. So Morell, perhaps reverting back in his thinking to his Berlin practice and happier days, tried useless but harmless tissue extracts. Several drugs which contained vitamins were prescribed and though the total dose of vitamin was excessive, no signs of toxicity developed. It should also be noted that contrary to the statements in the report of Morell's interrogation (see Appendix C), intravenous glucose is not a source of significant nourishment and it has no psychological effect. The use of antibacterial drugs, sulpha and penicillin, are self-explanatory. Morell's use of sulpha to prevent colds and infection was questionable by the standards of that day, but not grossly erroneous, and German medicine had had no research experience with penicillin.

We now turn to methamphetamine,* a drug not on Morell's list, but one which Hitler was surely taking both orally and intravenously with deadly effects. The evidence supporting those assertions begins with our interview with Heinz Linge, Hitler's *Kammerdiener* from 1935 to the end. The nearest English equivalent to *Kammerdiener* is 'valet', which is how we have described him. But Linge, a military officer, had broader duties. He was in charge of Hitler's quarters and of his personal bodyguard. We found him a burly, friendly man who received us cordially. He had been taken prisoner by the Russians after the collapse of the German defence of Berlin and spent ten years in their prison camps. He is now apparently a prospering small contractor. He acknowledges Hitler's errors of judgement but still looks for ways to loyally defend him in statements such as, 'He wanted only good for Germany'. Overall, he impressed us as a truthful, uncomplicated man whose military background was still evident in his bearing and his responses.

Linge told us that starting in late 1941 or early 1942, Hitler received an intravenous injection from Morell nearly every morning before he got out of bed. That Morell did see Hitler nearly every morning, usually before breakfast, is confirmed by the

---

* Methamphetamine was the version of amphetamine developed in Germany. It is a member of the amphetamine group and is of about the same pharmacologic potency as dextro-amphetamine (Dexedrine) which was in common use in England and the USA.

appointment book Linge kept at the time.[14] The injection was not given because Hitler was in pain or experiencing any particular distress, but rather it was given simply as a routine part of the preparation for the day. One ampoule which was always used was labelled Vitamultin-Ca, an injectable form of the vitamin preparation manufactured at the Hamma factory. It is included in Morell's list of drugs. The critical data are supplied in descriptions of what happened when the drug was injected. Linge clearly remembers that the effects were instantly apparent—not minutes later, but while the needle was still in the arm. The effect on Hitler was obviously alerting: he felt 'fresh', alert, active, and immediately ready for the day.[15] The purpose of the injection was obviously to energize. Linge's main point is confirmed by Russian medical authorities who stated on the basis of their intelligence that Hitler had a 'pep' injection every morning.[16] Later in the war, probably starting in the middle of 1943, Hitler began to get injections at other times of the day. There were many witnesses to these injections and all concur as to the effects. Himmler had noted that Morell's injections made Hitler 'immediately' alert and active and both he and Dr Brandt believed that the immediacy of the alerting effect was what so impressed Hitler about Morell's injections.[17] Traudl Junge, one of Hitler's secretaries, also told us that the effect of the injections was immediate and that Hitler became extremely alert and talkative. Assmann, too, described the effect as immediate and 'rejuvenating'.[18] Walter Hewel, who was a representative of the foreign office on Hitler's staff and a member of Hitler's inner circle, said that Hitler called for Morell more and more often, especially when bad news came in. Hewel recalled that after the injection, Hitler became cheerful, talkative, physically active and tended to stay awake long hours into the night.[19]

These descriptions provide critical evidence. The effects described by Linge and the other witnesses are characteristic of an injection of a stimulant drug of the amphetamine group or cocaine, and are not compatible with any other active drug. Amphetamines and cocaine are so similar pharmacologically that it matters little which one was used, but amphetamine is much

Adolf Hitler and Dr. Morrell (*National Archives*)

Dr. Theo Morrell after receiving the *Ritterkreuz* (the Knight's Cross) from Hitler, 1944 *(National Archives)*

more probable because its injectable form was readily available, while injectable cocaine was an illegal drug and among its users sniffing was the preferred method of administration. Also, the effects of amphetamine last two or three hours, while the action of cocaine is much more rapidly terminated. The effects on Hitler were relatively long-lasting.

The only plausible alternative to a stimulant of the amphetamine or cocaine class would be that the injection contained no active drug at all, but rather was a placebo. Morell hardly would have dared to deliberately give a placebo, but any one of his useless nostrums could have served such a purpose. Evidence against the possibility of a placebo is the duration of the administrations which extended over at least four years. Usually the effect of a placebo decreases drastically after a few treatments. There will be much more evidence against the placebo alternative to come, but no one with experience in medicine would exclude the possibility entirely at this point. Hitler was either treated with a stimulant or placebo. The evidence so far can be explained in no other way.

For further evidence strongly favouring amphetamine we return briefly to the notion of tolerance which, as noted earlier, several observers commented upon. Morell himself said of the morning injections that he had to increase the dose 'from 2 to 4 to 10 to 16 cc's' (cubic centimetres) in order to get an effect.[20] Of the drugs capable of producing tolerance, alcohol can be eliminated. Except for an occasional beer, Hitler abstained from alcohol and was virtually a teetotaller. The remaining possibilities are short-acting barbiturates, Eukodal or another narcotic, and amphetamine or a similar stimulant. The same classes of drugs, and only these classes among drugs available at that time, produce the instantaneous sense of pleasurable well-being that Linge and others described—the 'rush' or 'flash' in the jargon of the street addict. Narcotics and barbiturates characteristically produce intense, joyful relaxation and a dreamy state. Only amphetamine or related stimulants produce arousal compatible with the evidence from observers.

The repeated injections may have had a special psychological consequence because intravenous injections of drugs producing instantaneous pleasurable sensations are associated with a sort of conditioning. This is reported in particular by narcotic addicts for whom the mere sight of the needle and other accoutrements needed for a 'fix' is sufficient to elicit pleasurable sensations similar to, though usually less intense, than those felt when the drug is actually injected. Many addicts make an elaborate ritual out of the preparations for administration of a drug, thereby prolonging and intensifying the pleasure. While no direct evidence is available, something like this may well have happened between Hitler and Morell. Morell steadily increased the number of injections Hitler received until the total reached two to five daily (see Appendix C). 'Herr Reich Injektion Minister' the orotund Göring teased Morell. But why did Hitler tolerate repeated injections, especially since oral administration of most drugs used would have been fully effective? The insertion of a needle into a vein is at best uncomfortable, and Hitler would have insisted on knowing exactly what purpose the injections were serving. Conditioning to the needle is a plausible explanation for the inordinate use of it.

Amphetamine was almost certainly present in another form of Vitamultin which came in tablets for oral use. The preparation made for Hitler was for his use only and came wrapped in gold foil to distinguish it from all other preparations. Hitler took up to ten such tablets daily, but a more typical dose would have been four to five.[21] He is described during his last years as often fumbling with vitamin tablets during military conferences and taking one or two. In 1943 a chemical analysis of a gold-wrapped Vitamultin tablet was done.

Professor Ernst-Günther Schenck was, in 1943, a nutrition inspector for the Waffen SS and the Wehrmacht. Already Germany was suffering severe shortages of raw materials including those used for vitamin production. There was real malnutrition and conditions were getting worse. Despite the shortages, Morell seemed able to maintain production. Dr Schenck was curious about Morell's product and mildly suspicious that it might be either diluted with inert ingredients or possibly wastefully over-concentrated. He also wanted to find out, if possible, the source of the ingredients used. He surreptitiously obtained one of the gold-wrapped tablets, ground it up to prevent identification by its shape, and sent it to one of the laboratories in the Nutrition Inspector's office for analysis of its vitamin content. The report came back and revealed that the tablet contained the vitamins as stated. But in addition to the vitamins, it also contained Pervitin, a brand name for methamphetamine, and caffeine. Dr Schenck showed the report to Dr Leonardo Conti, Reich Health Leader, and the head of the German health bureaucracy. Conti told Himmler, who replied with instructions to contact Schenck to drop the entire matter. Dr Schenck obediently destroyed the report. Today he does not remember the name of the chemist who did the analysis or the reported concentration of methamphetamine. After the war, Dr Schenck spent ten years in a Russian prison camp and after his release, told his story to Dr H. D. Röhrs, who published it.[22] Later, in connection with a civil law suit, Dr Schenck told the same story under oath.

Is Schenck's story credible? Conti and Himmler are dead, so it cannot be independently verified. Dr Schenck himself is still active in medicine, mainly in pharmacological and nutritional research. When we interviewed him, he was most responsive and gave every appearance of a man of integrity. He has published scientific papers, mainly in nutrition, and his scientific reputation is unblemished. There are also clues to his character in an extraordinarily interesting book he wrote about his experiences in Berlin at the time of the city's fall to the Russian armies.[23] At first he was in charge of public health in the city which involved obtaining and distributing food, water, and medical supplies, as well as trying to stop epidemic diseases which continually threatened. Later he was for several days the last active physician in Hitler's headquarters bunker, caring for the sick and wounded who crowded in as the Russian armies pressed closer. Although the book is a sparsely factual account of events, Dr Schenck does stand out as an energetic man who was selflessly dedicated to public health and medicine. That is also the course his career has followed. There seems to be simply nothing about him to raise doubt. Moreover, and perhaps as important, the analysis of Vitamultin was quite feasible. German chemistry was very advanced and a competent chemist presented with a powder to assay for vitamin content would have noted an unknown substance in the course of a routine examination and would have identified it. Detection and identification of methamphetamine was not unduly problematic so the technical requirements of Schenck's story are easily met. We conclude therefore, that there is no reason to doubt Dr Schenck and that Hitler was indeed taking methamphetamine orally as well as intravenously.

An important drug interaction was also likely a factor in the total picture. Caffeine, itself a weak stimulant drug, significantly augments the effects of amphetamine. Hitler hardly used coffee or tea, the usual sources of caffeine, but through the day he did continuously suck on a hard cola candy (such as Cola-Dalmann) which did contain caffeine. Hitler used such large amounts of cola candy that he no doubt got an effective pharmacologic dose

The evidence cited builds an extremely strong circumstantial case that Hitler was receiving amphetamines orally and intravenously. However, absolutely excluding placebo and obtaining more exact information about the times during which he was using greater or lesser amounts of drug would be desirable. We tried hard to find such evidence and did find a few pieces which fit in neatly with what has been set forth. But we also followed dead ends which are worth describing so that future scholarly investigations will be better able to get on to profitable paths.

One aim of our investigation was to trace Morell's sources of drugs. The Morell microfilms clearly establish that until the assassination attempt in July 1944, drugs came to Führer Hauptquartier through a single pharmacy, the Engel Apotheke in Berlin. Both of the pharmacists who worked through that period are dead, and in fact, one died just three weeks before we attempted to contact him. Unfortunately, all business records were destroyed during the battle for Berlin. Through the widow of one of the pharmacists, we did, however, locate a woman who had worked in the Engel Apotheke as a clerk and janitor. She remembered regular deliveries from Engle Apotheke to Führer Hauptquartier, but could not remember any specific drugs. She was quite sure that none of the drugs involved was actually compounded into its final form in the Apotheke—at least not routinely. Thus, it is unlikely that metamphetamine was added to Vitamultin at the pharmacy. Morell's correspondence shows that the pharmacy received Vitamultin directly from the Hamma factory. Hence, the final preparation must have been compounded at the factory, which is logical for another reason. Morell owned Hamma and thus had control over its employees. One of those employees was Dr Kurt Mulli, the chief chemist, but Morell and Mulli were much more to each other than employer-employee. They were close personal friends, as was demonstrated on several occasions, but most clearly when late in the war, Morell gave Mulli written authority to take charge of all of his financial affairs.[24] The Morell microfilms clearly establish that Mulli personally made up a 'special' preparation of Vitamultin in his own home for which he had to have permission from local officials.[25] Morell helped him secure the permission. Of course, we wanted very much to interview Dr Mulli, and wrote several letters to him which were not answered. Dr Mulli died in April 1977, one week before we had planned to arrive at his doorstep unannounced. In 1978 we tried to contact his wife, but she also proved unapproachable. The Mullis were the only people to whom we wrote who would not see us and co-operate with our medical investigation, except for one woman who was ill. They were the only persons who did not answer letters.

The evidence leads us to conclude that most likely Mulli mixed methamphetamine with injectable Vitamultin Ca and Vitamultin F tablets. But if so, why such a circuitous route to obtain the drug? Because of crashes of Luftwaffe aircraft due to errors of pilots who were using amphetamine, Germany in 1941 became one of the first nations to regulate amphetamine under narcotic laws. Of course, Morell could still have obtained the drug for Hitler, but not without bypassing the drug control authorities, and that could not have been done without attracting attention, and it surely would not have been easy. The bureaucracy was extremely thorough, efficient, and persistent. Even Hermann Göring, the second most powerful man in Germany, had real difficulty obtaining narcotics (morphine) to which he had become addicted during his treatment for a painful wound. Berlin pharmacists would not co-operate with the ruses that he had used to obtain the drug.[26] Göring's attempts to obtain narcotics from overseas, from military sources and through medical channels made his addiction notorious. Obviously, the problem for Morell and Hitler was to obtain methamphetamine without invoking Hitler's name. Moreover, methamphetamine marketed as Pervitin was ubiquitous in Germany. If Hitler had used the drug freely in his headquarters, the name would have been recognized and Hitler's image would have suffered. Even the tablets would have been recognized. Having the drug compounded by the Hamma factory and disguised in vitamin preparations was surely the easiest path to follow. Even at that there actually were continual difficulties between Morell, Hamma and the Engel Apotheke which involved the narcotic laws. The letters in the Morell microfilms are cryptic—much of the business must have been done by telephone or during personal contacts, but there was clearly concern at the Apotheke about maintaining narcotics records and a definite air of conspiracy in the letters.[27] If, as we think, this was the course of events, there is a further implication: Hitler had planned on using amphetamine frequently if not continuously.

There was one major challenge to Morell during the time in which he attended Hitler. This was mounted by the other physicians in Hitler's entourage. Two surgeons, Drs Karl Brandt and Hans Karl von Hasselbach, travelled with Hitler in order to be available should a surgical emergency occur. Both heartily disliked Morell, but Morell was definitely in charge. He alone asked for consultations, and, in fact, until the assassination attempt, neither surgeon had a real chance to examine Hitler. But after the attempt, Dr von Hasselbach was first to arrive at the scene and treated Hitler's superficial injuries. Because of the ruptured eardrums, Dr Giesing, the otolaryngologist, was called. He arrived on 22 July, and Morell, according to Giesing, was angry. In his statement to American interrogators, Giesing quoted Morell: 'Who are you, I alone get consultants'.[28] Morell 'scolded' Giesing for attending Hitler without his permission, was 'very nasty', stating repeatedly that Hitler was his 'personal responsibility and no one could touch him without his permission'. But the injured eardrums forced the issue and Morell acceded.

Giesing, who had seen Hitler only at a distance before, had an opportunity to examine him and then, because of the infection which developed, stayed on for three months. Finally, troubled by Hitler's mental state and general condition, Giesing acted. Noticing that there were six strange black pills on Hitler's breakfast tray, Giesing searched through Morell's drug supplies and found the black pills with their descriptive literature, Dr Koester's Antigas Pills. This was on 3 October 1944, just as Hitler was recovering from his jaundice and hence, at a time when Morell had likely suspended any questionable drug treatments. The liver metabolizes drugs and therefore, any physician would be extra-cautious when liver function is impaired. So it was a very inopportune time for an investigation, but Giesing was struck by the strychnine content of Dr Koester's pills. Strychnine was, after all, a notorious poison and since he knew that some toxic substances do accumulate, causing strange medical syndromes, perhaps strychnine would explain Hitler's illness, which was indeed strange. He talked to Brandt and von Hasselbach: both had become alarmed by Hitler's deterioration and both accepted strychnine as a probable cause. A glimpse into the medical literature might have saved the three of them serious trouble, but there was no medical library at Führer Hauptquartier. Morell kept only one medical text, *Frank's Moderne Therapie*, a brief synopsis of medicine similar to *Merck's Manual*.[29] Having decided to act, Brandt first tried to reason with Morell, arguing that the episode of jaundice was a threat to all the doctors, and asking that Morell tell them about the treatments he was using. Morell's perception is recorded in a note he made at the time.[30]

Talk with Brandt. He (Brandt) said, 'Do you think anyone would believe you if you would say that you only follow orders?

Do you think that Himmler would treat you better than anyone else? Right now so many people are getting hanged, the whole matter would have been judged very coldly. If something would have happened to the Führer, can you imagine what would have followed? One wouldn't have held von Hasselbach responsible, but you and most probably I would have been. Therefore, it is best if from now on I always know what is going on here.'

Morell did not record his verbatim response, but it must have been negative, because Brandt went directly to Hitler and on 10 October, Hitler summoned Morell, Brandt, von Hasselbach and Giesing. Himmler and Bormann were also present. Afterward Morell, obviously upset, wrote:[31]

von Hasselbach admitted that they wanted to get rid of me. Dr. Giesing saw the box with the drug preparations and read the description and therefore saw strychnine in the composition. Giesing told von Hasselbach, who became excited and told Brandt. Then came the most underhanded attack against me in order to get rid of me.

But the attack failed. Saying that he had taken Dr Koester's pills for years, long before he had met Morell, and that squabbling doctors were no use to him, Hitler discharged Brandt, Giesing and von Hasselbach.

Though rid of physicians looking over his shoulder, Morell was still searching for a cause of the jaundice and Hitler's general decline. So was Hitler or possibly someone else in authority, such as Himmler. Three letters from Morell to Dr Mulli illustrate the thinking at Führer Hauptquartier. On 30 September 1944, during the jaundice, Morell asked Mulli for analysis of Brom-Nervacit, one of the sedatives used by Hitler, 'for gas-forming or fermenting impurities'. An answer in writing was demanded.[32] On 9 October, Morell asked Mulli for an analysis of a sample of tap water for 'bacteria and any chemicals'. This time a written answer was not specified.[33] Then on 11 October, the day after the firing of the doctors, Morell sent Mulli a sample of urine with instructions to analyse it for strychnine. Again, a written answer was demanded.[34] We did not find Mulli's written answers to the specific questions in the records, but Morell recorded a telephone call he made to Mulli on 10 October, during which he asked about the results, and there is a letter of 28 November from Mulli, obviously written in response to Morell's problems, in which Mulli gives Morell advice about treatment of Hitler; it was a calming, supportive letter.[35]

The failure of Hitler's doctors is a story replete with irony and it is not yet finished. Dr Giesing, the main instigator of the confrontation with Morell, had the essential clue that might have led to a correct diagnosis, but he did not recognize its importance. While treating Hitler after the assassination attempt for his injuries and later for ear, sinus, and pharyngeal infections, Giesing used topical cocaine in a 10 per cent solution as a local anaesthetic and to reduce the swelling of tissues (see Appendix C). Painting cocaine on to mucous membranes was (and is) standard medical practice for those purposes, but Hitler's response was quite unusual. He seemed to enjoy the treatment, asked for it so often that Giesing became reluctant to administer it; he even requested that the concentration of drug be increased.[36] Other evidence already presented, such as the improvement in the tremor, suggests that during this period, late July and early August 1944, amphetamine was not being administered and Hitler was withdrawing from it. Now cocaine and amphetamine had virtually identical effects, but the pharmacology is very subtle so that a simple substitution of cocaine for amphetamine will not explain the observations. One obvious problem is dosage, because cocaine is about the same potency as amphetamine, or not quite as potent, and it is at first hard to see how Hitler could have obtained sufficient amounts of the drug from topical applications to ward off withdrawal. Moreover, the same response from Hitler was obtained later from eyedrops containing 1 per cent cocaine, which would deliver an even smaller dose. To explain the data and Dr Giesing's missed opportunity, we will have to go rather deeply into the pharmacology of these two most engrossing drugs.

Medical Treatment

The extent to which cocaine may have been substituting for amphetamine, and thus relieving the symptoms of withdrawal, must be explored. For example, a barbiturate will prevent withdrawal from a drug such as benzodiazapine (e.g. valium). Another closely related phenomenon is the hypersensitivity which develops during withdrawal, allowing extremely low doses of the drug being withdrawn (or one substituting for it) to cause an exaggerated response. For example, any one who has stopped smoking for a few hours, and is in early withdrawal, and then has inhaled deeply on a cigarette will know the response. After day or two of withdrawal, even sitting next to a smoker and getting second-hand whiffs, will serve the same purpose. Now amphetamine and cocaine have identical effects, but they achieve those effects through different modes of action; the same result reached by different pathways. But a peculiar property of both drugs has prevented pharmacologists from studying them systematically for cross-tolerance. Unlike sedatives or narcotic drugs, which when withdrawn produce observable signs, the effect of withdrawal from stimulants is mainly depression, a subjective state which cannot be measured in experimental animals. Only very recently have techniques been developed which have permitted the study of the effects of substituting amphetamine for cocaine in animals.[37] Cross-tolerance does clearly develop, but the studies proving this are too new to have been followed up with others investigating the finer details of the interaction.

Another standard investigative procedure is to ask questions of human users. Under controlled conditions, persons given cocaine or amphetamine intravenously cannot distinguish between the two drugs—the subjective effects are identical—except that the effects of amphetamines are longer lasting.[38] Patients we have treated say two pertinent things: amphetamine and cocaine together give a combined effect greater than either drug alone and that cocaine will prevent the withdrawal symptoms from amphetamine although it is not a perfect substitute.

All this evidence clearly supports the existence of cross-tolerance which would explain Giesing's observations, except for the apparent hypersensitivity to cocaine. That cocaine could produce this response in a person withdrawing from amphetamine is a very likely hypothesis which, so far as we know, has never been experimentally tested. It is also an extremely interesting hypothesis which today, thirty-four years after Giesing treated Hitler in the Führer's bunker, is right on the cutting edge of psychopharmacological research.

Giesing, of course, could have known only that amphetamine and cocaine had virtually identical effects. But he describes being sufficiently puzzled by an unusual reaction to cocaine which could well have led him to think further into the problem instead of pursuing the fruitless lead presented by Dr Koester's pills. Of course, reaching hypotheses that might have led eventually to a correct diagnosis would have required inspired genius with few parallels in medical history. But the critical clue was available.

After the doctors' confrontation, Morell stayed on with Hitler and there is no evidence of significant change in Morell's treatment. Dr Ludwig Stumpfegger, a surgeon in the SS, was attached to Führer Hauptquartier in case of need. On 22 April 1945, with Russian armies already invading Berlin, Morell fled. This was the day that Hitler decided to stay in Berlin, and Morell later told his American interrogators that he wanted to give Hitler morphine to calm him, but that Hitler refused treatment and dismissed Morell saying that he had no more need of Morell's drugs. Hitler had always publicly made a point of never exposing himself knowingly to addicting drugs and morphine was the example he usually cited. Other witnesses say that Morell whined and begged to be allowed to leave. Either way, he did succeed in getting out of Berlin and into a hospital at Bad Reichenhall in the far south of Germany, and far away from Russians. A curious event then occurred which was described by Dr Rolf Makkus, then Morell's adjutant, and currently an attorney. Dr Makkus was surprised that we had located him, but was co-operative and seemed to be a dependable witness. He had accompanied Morell from Berlin and the party carried with them a German army footlocker containing records of Morell's treatment of Hitler, Mussolini, and Hacha, the president of Czechoslovakia. Makkus insisted that Morell did keep detailed records consistent with his meticulous business correspondence. Bad Reichenhall was not yet occupied, but in those last days of the war, the confusion was such that no area was secure. Morell was terrified, a physical coward according to Makkus, and he had Makkus inter the footlocker in a stone wall which surrounded a field, and seal it in with rocks and cement. A few days later, French troops arrived and Morell, petrified with fear, told them where the footlocker was hidden before any questions were asked. Morell led a party of soldiers who were accompanied by an American woman working as a war correspondent (or so Makkus thinks) to the spot and turned the footlocker over to them. He has heard nothing more of the matter, but thinks that those records would be critically important to a quantitative evaluation of Hitler's treatment. We agree and have queried French and American archives.[39] No one seems to have the footlocker or the records. No such item is listed among Morell's possessions when he came into American custody. It may be lying about unindexed in the storage facility of some government, or it may be in private hands. Perhaps it became part of the flotsam of war and has been lost.

Morell soon passed into American hands and, after an interrogation at Bad Reichenhall, was sent to the Military Intelligence Service Center or 'Ashcan'. He made a disgusting impression on the Americans. In the introduction to his interrogations he is described as . . . 'one of the most unwholesome persons this centre has housed' and by another American:

> Dr Morell has been the subject of a large number of interrogation reports all of which refer to him in a most uncomplimentary manner. Some reports describe him as a shrewd, money-crazed quack doctor who believes in his own quackery; others describe his hygienic habits as being those of a pig. This interrogator has very little to add and can only agree.[40]

Those descriptions are somewhat overdrawn in that Morell was, after all, a prisoner, and apparently ill with some sort of cardiopulmonary problem. He was interrogated by American

intelligence officers, but not very intensely or very skilfully and not
until September 1945, when he had recovered from his illness and
was no doubt better able to weigh his answers. The original notes
handwritten in English from which the interrogation report was
obviously written were somehow included in the Morell papers.
They suggest sketchy questions with little probing.[41] It does
appear that a physician organized the questioning though the
final report was signed by a 2nd Lieutenant of infantry. Excepting
Stumpfegger, who was killed in Berlin, all of the German doctors
who had known Hitler were assembled at 'Ashcan'. Morell was
assigned to share a room with Brandt. In general, the German
doctors regarded the prisoner-of-war camps as not such bad
places to be in those hectic days, and so when the Americans
asked them to write out their responses to several general questions, they did so, spinning out their replies at great length.
'Useless, but it kept us busy,' von Hasselbach told us.[42] But war
crimes charges by the Allies and exchange of recriminations
among the Germans were in the air and the doctors were guarded.
So, no doubt, was Morell and he said nothing about gold-
wrapped Vitamultin or Pervitin. The doctors were soon released
and went their separate ways. Morell gathered up the considerable remains of his business and lived out his life in Bavaria. But
he never recovered his health and died in 1948. Giesing and von
Hasselbach returned to medical practice and are still active.
Brandt suffered a tragic fate. After being fired by Hitler, he had
been named Reich Commissioner for sanitation and health. Then
on 16 April 1945, he was arrested on Hitler's personal order and
charged with moving his family from Berlin to Bad Liebenstein
where they would be in an area occupied by Americans. Hitler
had forbidden such movements out of the eastern areas. The next
day he was sentenced to death, but the execution was stayed from
day to day because, Brandt thought, the authorities were going to
try to get him to implicate colleagues on the same charge. The
delays continued until after Hitler's death, and then Brandt's
close friend, Albert Speer, got him released. But he was soon
charged by the Americans with responsibility for medical experiments and was tried by a War Crimes Tribunal. The basis of the

charge had been his position as Reich Commissioner, which he held, it seems, only nominally; his defence was he had no authority or responsibility over the facilities and personnel specified in the charge which was surely true, but Brandt was sentenced to death. He offered to undergo the same medical experiments himself, but was refused and was executed by hanging.

CHAPTER SIX

Amphetamines

We must now temporarily leave Hitler in order to present factual background about amphetamine. Historians and general readers who wish to understand more about Hitler need access to the pertinent facts about this drug which, with or without Hitler, is fascinating in its own right. Even physicians, who would of course know in a general way that amphetamine could cause some of the signs and symptoms exhibited by Hitler, would have to turn to their textbooks and periodicals to get a more comprehensive picture.

The history of the amphetamine drugs is short but colourful. Their pharmacologic properties were explored in the 1920s and 1930s and they were first reported to be effective central nervous system stimulants in 1935. Amphetamines belong to a class of drugs, the sympathomimetics, which stimulate the sympathetic nervous system but are set apart from most other drugs in that class, such as adrenaline, because they produce greater effects on the brain than on the peripheral nervous system. The effects of moderate doses are dramatic. Alertness is increased and fatigue decreased. An arousal response can be seen on the electroencephalogram and can be measured by increased motor activity and improved performance on some tests of motor skill, including some athletic events. Mood is elevated often to euphoric levels: most people like the effects. There is increased spontaneity, initiative, confidence and sense of well-being. Appetite is suppressed and the apparent need for sleep is lessened. Amphetamine is classed as a reinforcing drug because mammals will do work if access to the drug is a result and will increase their work as needed to obtain increasing amounts of the drug. Side-effects are minor. There are increases, usually small ones, in heart rate and blood pressure but the main side-effects from moderate doses are only insomnia when arousal is not wanted, and appetite suppression when that effect is not wanted. It was a dramatic drug which attracted world-wide attention from the time it was first introduced into medicine. Tabloid newspapers extolled it as a miracle drug, a banisher of fatigue, a maker of supermen capable of superhuman acts, and while the language of the medical press and of relatively sedate elements in the popular press was more restrained, the conclusions offered were hardly less enthusiastic. Dozens of brand names were registered and some can now be found in any large dictionary: Dexedrine, Benzedrine, Methedrine, Desoxyn and, in Germany, Pervitin. The drug was so well known that 'Benny' (for benzedrine) became popular slang. Amphetamines were often treated humorously, such as in an American popular song of the 1940s, 'Who put the Benzedrine in Mrs Murphey's Ovaltine?'

Although amphetamine was first marketed as a specific treatment for a rare disorder (narcolepsy), and there are other medical uses, its major use was to produce arousal, and mood elevation or appetite reduction; one effect, or sometimes two, and sometimes all three were sought by normal people unaffected by any disease. As early as 1936, American medical students were using Dexedrine in order to stay awake for study. Truck drivers soon learned the same pharmacology. All of the major belligerent nations in World War II experimented with amphetamine and all of them issued the drug to military units. A German Panzer veteran told us. 'When we missed sleep we ate Pervitin like candy; without it we couldn't have done what we did'. In civilian medicine the amphetamines were used as stimulants and anti-depressants but their main application, at least nominally, was for appetitie suppression. Weight reduction clinics were established all across America dispensing amphetamines in huge amounts.

That amphetamines were dangerous, even deadly, was not widely acknowledged until recently. Since 1936 there had been sporadic case reports in the medical literature describing alarming toxic symptoms, but the drug was so popular and apparently so safe for most people that the defenders of it remained a strong majority. As late as 1958 a renowned academic pharmacologist published a monograph favourable to the amphetamines and in that year, in America, twenty doses of amphetamine were produced for every man, woman, and child in the nation. The increasing number of adverse case reports continued to be dismissed as isolated, idiosyncratic reactions. It took the world-wide drug abuse epidemic of the 1960s to strip away the blindfolds.

Tolerance occurs to all the important actions of amphetamine and because of tolerance the dosage must be increased in order to maintain the desired effects. Appetite suppression is lost by about ten days if the dose is not increased and by four to six weeks if the dosage is moderately increased. Mood elevation decreases because of tolerance at about the same rate or even more rapidly. When the dose is increased to overcome tolerance, sooner or later toxicity will appear. However, the toxic effects of amphetamine at constant dosages vary greatly between individuals. Many persons have used large daily doses for years without any untoward effects at all. But there are also rare instances of toxic psychoses from a single moderate dose. Most persons fall somewhere between those extremes. The essential point is that toxicity is correlated better with individual variation in susceptibility than with dosage. Practically speaking, if the dose is increased to overcome tolerance, any user of amphetamine will cross his particular threshold and toxicity will appear.

There are two fairly distinct patterns of overuse, one based on oral intake and the other on intravenous injection. The initial motivation for using the drug, not the outcome, is the basic difference between these types of users. Oral users, generally seeking weight reduction or arousal, but at the same time receiving the reinforcing euphoria, at first obtained the desired effects plus a few others generally regarded as negative: distractability, restlessness, motor hyperactivity, talkativeness and dry mouth. Merging with these and becoming more prominent as the dosage is increased are other more ominous ones: suspiciousness, agitation, loss of emotional control, impulsiveness, irritability, and an over-elated mood with consequent impaired judgement. Elevated mood affects judgement because unrealistic optimism leads to misassessment of the environment and mistaken decisions. Thinking becomes rigid, over-concerned with details, or narrowly fixed on one or two general subjects with exclusion or inattention to other ideas. These effects are especially noticeable when the intellectual task confronting the user is complex with many ramifications and alternatives to consider. An old saw of pharmacology says that 'amphetamines produce constipation of the mind and diarrhoea of the mouth'. There are also physical signs associated with amphetamine toxicity including weight loss, gross tremor (especially of the limbs and sometimes of the tongue), increased muscle tone (especially of the trunk) and facial twitching and tics. If the development of toxicity continues, the usual outcome is a confused state in which orientation (recognition of time and place) is mildly impaired and the affected person seems vague, easily distractable, and unsure. At the same time there is imprecise thinking resulting in rambling unclear speech, delusions, usually of persecution, and sometimes hallucinations of hearing, taste, smell, or touch. Memory is unimpaired but failure of concentration may simulate a deficit. If the confusion is minimal and does not dominate the picture the final stages are much like paranoid schizophrenia. The toxic and psychotic behaviours tend to vary from hour to hour, sometimes related to events in the external environment, sometimes with no apparent connection. In addition, progression to the severest toxicity is rather rare. Most users maintain themselves within a limited range of the toxic continuum for extended periods. In these ways the drug can produce an extremely puzzling and distressing picture for those observing the affected person. A knowledgeable researcher in the field said that 'no other group of drugs can affect or change character and personality traits to a degree greater than the amphetamines'.[1]

Amphetamine abuse by intravenous injection of methamphetamine was first practised by large numbers of people in Japan just after World War II when military stockpiles of the drug appeared on the black market. A major epidemic followed which had spread to the United States and Europe by the 1960s. Young adults were the victims. Methamphetamine, called 'speed' or 'flash' by the denizens of the drug culture, given intravenously produced an immediate and intensely pleasurable sensation often likened to sexual orgasm. Also, there was an intense feeling of physical and mental competence. Fatigue, depression, doubt, and pessimism were banished by drug. Euphoria, optimism, volubility, and invulnerability appeared instantaneously. Many users repeated the injection every three or four hours for several days, a 'run', until the 'crash', which was a day or two of profound sleep.

The toxic effects from the intravenous use are much the same as when the use is predominantly oral except that the time between administration and the appearance of toxicity is compressed. Within minutes of an injection, suspiciousness, hyperactivity, delusions of persecution and so on may appear. There are in addition other toxic effects which appear with oral intake but are exaggerated, and hence more easily described when the intake is intravenous. These include several curious behaviours called stereotypes, i.e., actions that are repeated over and over again. Cleaning objects or arranging and rearranging them in meticulous detail, repeated gnawing movements of the jaws or actual biting of some object, or picking at the skin are typical examples. An odd jerking of the extremities or of the facial muscles, repeated but not rhythmical, sometimes appears. Finally, because intravenous administration produces a sudden constriction of muscles controlling blood flow in small arteries, many intravenous users suffer occlusions of small arteries, especially of the kidneys, gut, heart, brain, and eye. Recent autopsy studies have found such vascular occlusion to be far commoner than had been thought.[2] The constriction of small vessels produces a rapid rise in blood pressure which may lead to vascular catastrophe involving major arteries. During the last decade, several deaths due to stroke have been reported.[3] And of special significance to the story of Hitler, some intravenous users report severe crushing chest pain accompanied by feelings of impending death which occurs during or immediately following an intravenous injection. This particular effect is not prominently mentioned in medical literature, but users say it is fairly common, especially towards the end of a series of 'runs'.

Within a day or two of stopping administration of the drug, the disturbances of thinking and emotionality return to normal in most cases. Rarely will those problems persist for longer periods and then usually in persons with notable pre-existing personality problems. However, withdrawal does produce a new set of troubles, in particular a depressed mood and, although whether or not amphetamine is addicting in the sense that physiological changes occur on withdrawal is controversial, the depression does in fact lead to taking more drug in order to obtain relief. Many chronic users take an intravenous dose in the morning in order to get started for the day. If the depression is allowed to run its course, it peaks in about four days and is often so severe and distressing that suicide is a significant risk. Although the depression usually lightens after a few more days, a chronic mild depression, excessive fatigue, and a feeling of reduced efficiency may persist for weeks.

Considerable effort has been expended trying to define a specific personality especially liable to overuse drugs. Obviously it would be helpful to physicians to be able to recognize vulnerable persons. But unhappily, while studies have found an apparent excess of persons with pre-existing neurotic and personality disorders among amphetamine abusers, there are also too many apparent normals in most series of cases to allow delimiting persons liable to drug abuse on the basis of personality. There is only one trait that does characterize a large proportion of amphetamine abusers, and that is previous abuse of other drugs.

CHAPTER SEVEN

Diagnoses

Diagnosis is the essential act of medicine because it makes possible the prediction of the future course of illness with and without available treatments. The accuracy of the prediction varies according to the inherent vicissitudes of particular disease processes and treatments: the natural course of measles is more predictable than tuberculosis; penicillin will cure syphilis while the outcome of surgery for lung cancer is much less certain. Because diagnosis will be important to understanding Adolf Hitler, a working grasp of the logic underlying the diagnostic process will be helpful.

Medicine has evolved a standard programme for arriving at a diagnosis which is based on the *differential diagnosis.* The procedure is that all of the facts related to the patient's current illness and medical history, in addition to any positive and negative findings from physical and laboratory examinations, are gathered and roughly organized with respect to the anatomic structures or organ systems seemingly involved in disease processes. Next, all of the afflictions which could possibly account for the data are named as possible diagnoses and the evidence for and against each one is set forth. Nearly always the evidence will exclude most diagnoses and allow implicit probabilities to be assigned to those remaining. When that is done, sometimes only one diagnosis will remain possible and occasionally two or three or more diagnoses will be more or less equally probable. But usually only one diagnosis, the *working diagnosis,* will be highly probable, and one or two additional diagnoses will remain possible. Laboratory tests, further examinations, and even trials of treatment are done to confirm or exclude possibilities until only one is tenable given the evidence. While measures capable of demonstrating specific

104

causes have become increasingly available, it is important to understand that the basic process remains the enumeration of *all* possible causes of a given set of medical facts followed by sequential elimination until only one remains.

If all of biology and human psychology were comprehended by this process, computers could make diagnoses. But computers fail because often enough even the science of modern medicine is unequal to the biological and personal idiosyncrasies of the individual who is ill. The judgement of the physician must then take over. Moreover, in the practical world, physicians can quickly sort out the irrelevant and misleading with efficiency which computers have not achieved.

While in the case of Adolf Hitler, we have assembled a reasonably complete medical history, the recorded observations of his physical condition are at best only passable. Any doctor could provide working diagnoses for each affected organ system, but needed laboratory and X-ray examinations are lacking. However, Hitler was observed over at least ten years and, as will be seen, that lengthy period of observation largely compensates for missing data.

The abdominal pain and jaundice, the two central features of Hitler's first illness, implicate the gastrointestinal system. When first presented with a complaint of abdominal pain the physician has many possibilities to consider. Visceral pain tends to be difficult to locate precisely, and quite different descriptions of the intensity and quality of their pain can come from persons with the same disease process involving the same organ. Given Hitler's initial complaints as they were recorded, one would have to consider disorders of most abdominal organs, the heart, the lungs, and the emotions. However, over the ten-year period of observation, the pain stayed about the same in quality and because there was no progression of disease in organs that would at first have to be suspected, many possibilities are excluded. Jaundice is the result of the deposition in the skin of bilirubin, a product of the breakdown of haemoglobin. As red blood cells are destroyed (they survive an average of 120 days), the oxygen-carrying component, haeme, is split producing bilirubin. As blood passes through the

105

liver, bilirubin is separated out by liver cells, which change it slightly to make it water soluble and secrete it into the bile ducts. The bile moves through its ductal system towards the gallbladder, where most is stored until the stimulus provided by ingested food causes contraction of the gallbladder and the discharge of bile into the small intestine. In the small bowel, bilirubin facilitates absorption of ingested food and water. When it reaches the large bowel, bacteria change most of the bilirubin so that it itself can be resorbed and reused. There are three basic ways that this elegant biological cycle can go wrong causing excess bilirubin to be deposited in the skin: (1) there can be excessive destruction of red blood cells overloading the system; (2) the liver cells, because of acquired or genetic disease, may be unable to process bilirubin from blood to bile; (3) there may be blockage in the bile ducts causing backup.

Hitler's pain was in the area occupied by the liver, the gallbladder, and the bile ducts. Sharp, cramping, intermittent pain is characteristic of obstruction of a hollow viscus or duct. Gallstones cause obstruction with pain and, if the obstruction is prolonged, jaundice. At Hitler's age, gallstones are common and are the most frequent cause of jaundice. There are also several lesser features of Hitler's illness adequately explained by gallstones. Because food intake stimulates activity of the gallbladder and ducts, pain from obstruction characteristically appears after meals. Gallbladder disease is associated with the sort of abdominal distension and belching about which Hitler complained. Change in diet is a typical first response of persons suffering from gallbladder disease; the rich fatty foods Hitler eliminated were typical too because they are the most powerful stimulants of the gallbladder. Fever and chills accompanied by severe colicky abdominal pain and vomiting, as experienced by Hitler in 1941, are commonly associated with gallstones because the obstruction leads to infection and the combination produces the signs and symptoms. Finally, it is not unusual for gallstones to produce signs and symptoms for years and yet progress no more than was the case with Hitler. One other observation is pertinent. Morell stated that Hitler's urine was dark brown 'at times', but he doesn't say which

106

times (see Appendix B). Dark brown urine, like the yellowing of the skin, is produced by bilirubin. If Morell's statement means that the 'times' were fairly widely separated, it is very strong evidence indeed favouring intermittent obstruction of bile flow as virtually nothing else would give that result. Hitler would certainly have had intermittent obstruction sufficient to cause bilirubin to spill over into the urine, but only once complete enough or prolonged enough to produce noticeable jaundice. Such a course is not uncommon.

The evidence against a diagnosis of gallstones with obstruction is this main fact: none of Hitler's doctor's appears to have considered that diagnosis. While only Morell was in a position to obtain and analyse the medical data, we would suppose that the others must have heard enough to arouse their suspicions. However, that apparently tells us more about the quality of his medical care than about his illness because Hitler did exhibit all of the major and minor signs and symptoms of a common medical syndrome, gallstones with intermittent obstruction of the biliary ducts causing episodic colicky pain with two major episodes of infection and one of jaundice. An example such as that could be from a textbook.

In order to explain the essential features of the abdominal illness in any other way at least two diagnoses will be required because the jaundice and the pain will have to be accounted for separately. Taking first the jaundice, Morell apparently thought that Hitler had viral hepatitis. He said that Hitler had 'gastroduodenitis with obstruction to bile flow', a descriptive phrase which was applied at that time to the illness later known as infectious hepatitis. It was thought that the bile ducts became involved in an inflammatory process that caused swelling and hence blockage of the ducts. In fact the direct effect of the illness on liver cells and lack of direct effect on the ductal system had been demonstrated about five years earlier but evidently Morell was not aware of that. Infectious hepatitis (hepatitis A) was endemic through the war years, and, although no one in contact with Hitler was known to have been affected, transmission to Hitler certainly could have occurred. Also, transmission of related viri (hepatitis B and C) occurs by hypodermic injection to which Hitler was certainly exposed, or through body secretions such as saliva. But in evidence against viral hepatitis are several critical facts. Hitler was old for hepatitis A which is mainly an illness of children and young adults. His jaundice, discovered while he was strolling in the sun outside his headquarters bunker, had been preceded by the abdominal cramps which were more frequent and intense, but he was otherwise in no particular distress. After it was discovered, the jaundice lasted only a few days, perhaps five at least, certainly no more than seven, but it is hard to ascertain because the observations which were recorded were made in the inadequate light available in the bunker. Now if viral hepatitis should produce jaundice, there is almost always a prodromal illness. For at least two days and more commonly for seven to fourteen days before the appearance of jaundice, fatigue and malaise are prominent. The victim is usually bedridden and obviously severely ill. After it appears, the jaundice persists for at least two, but usually four, weeks. The severe illness before the jaundice appears and the lengthy period before it disappears are so characteristic of hepatitis A that this diagnosis is incompatible with the evidence; hepatitis B or C, which do not produce such dramatic illness at the onset, are also most unlikely.

There are other possible causes of damage to liver cells with consequent jaundice. Toxins can produce liver damage, but nearly always other organs, such as the kidneys, would also be involved and there would be other signs of disease. None, however, were noted. Also, there was no history of exposure to known toxins. Some drugs produce liver injury through hypersensitivity reactions which are allergic in nature. However, this pathological mechanism would have produced a person sicker than Hitler seemed to be. The illness is due to an idiosyncratic response of the immune system and it is rare that the liver would be the only organ involved. (Though this is not true of drugs available today.) Generally there are other signs, such as skin rash and arthralgia (joint pains) for example, but none was noted. Also, hypersensitivity would recur the next time the offending agent was used, but there is no evidence that Morell changed Hitler's drug regimen and there followed no recurrence of the jaundice. There is no evidence at all to suggest increased destruction of red blood cells, and in fact there appears no plausible alternative to gallstones.

Also, an alternative explanation of the pain is difficult to find. Chronic pancreatitis, inflammation of the pancreas, is a remote possibility. The pain of pancreatitis is variable enough to account for what is known about the pain experienced by Hitler. However, by the time chronic pancreatitis has lasted ten years, enough pancreatic tissue usually has been destroyed to produce new signs and symptoms, such as diabetes or impaired digestion with loss of fat and protein and consequent weight loss. Hitler had no such signs. Also, chronic pancreatitis is usually associated with antecedent conditions, in particular alcoholism and gallstones. But as we have seen, Hitler used alcohol very sparingly, although it remains possible that gallstones produced some degree of pancreatitis late in the course of his illness.

There remains one further possibility to consider which is that the abdominal distress was due to disordered emotions. His doctors loosely ascribed his gastrointestinal pain, his tremor and his emotionality to 'hysteria' and those historians who have commented on Hitler's medical status have by and large accepted that explanation. Because of the wide currency given to a diagnosis of hysteria, we will have to consider the question in rather more detail than warranted by the evidence.

Hysteria has been used very imprecisely by both professionals and non-professionals. The psychiatric diagnosis is applied to a relatively discrete and easily identified syndrome beginning in adolescence or early adult life, featuring vividly described symptoms involving several organ systems and dramatic signs of illness: convulsions, paralysis of limbs, in fact, almost any medical condition can be simulated by hysteria. Hysteria has a characteristic emotional component, an over-dramatic description of symptoms coupled with a peculiar air of indifference, greatly increased suggestibility, and usually a gay light-hearted personality. Hysteria features multiple complaints that are vaguely described, often bizarre, and shift from one organ system to another. Hitler was so far from having any of these attributes that the diagnosis is just not tenable for him. Moreover, a ten-year history of a single relatively straightforward complaint would be at best extremely unusual in hysteria. Considering age of onset, the lack of any part of the behavioural syndrome, and the presence of behaviours that are incompatible with hysteria, forces dismissal of the diagnosis.

However, the argument does not really turn on the rejection of hysteria as defined in the psychiatric nomenclature. Through the years hysteria has been loosely applied to almost any unexplained symptom, and this seems to be the sense in which the term has been applied to Hitler. Experience has demonstrated this practice to be poor medicine because too often the 'hysterical' complaint later proved to be an early manifestation of major illness. However, there are psychological mechanisms which can result in medical symptoms and which must therefore be considered. First, there is flagrant malingering or feigning symptoms. Secondly, Hitler's pain might have been trivial but he exaggerated it: probably everyone has had the experience of finding small hurts a convenient excuse for a day off, or to avoid an unpleasant task, or to gain sympathy. That response can become pathologically exaggerated, and is then called hypochondriasis. Both malingering and hypochrondriasis are based on some sort of gain or advantage derived from the problematic behaviour: malingerers get disability compensation for example. Hitler, however, seems to have had nothing to gain at all. His pain got him no relief from his duties and he tended to hide it rather than exploit it. Nowhere in his personal relationships is there any hint of possible gain, either. In his recorded conversations, mention of medicine and symptoms is conspicuously rare. Malingering can surely be excluded, but there is a sense in which Hitler was hypochondriacal at times. Those times were associated with another psychological state: depression.

Depressed mood commonly leads to preoccupation with one's health and symptoms, a condition at times characteristic of Hitler. For example, the eye condition he developed in 1944 led him to say that he would soon go blind. It is likely that he was depressed at that time (see Chapter Two) and although imprecise dating makes definite association impossible, it appears that his hypochondriacal remarks were all attributable to depressed mood. There is also good evidence that he was not chronically hypochondriacal as would be the case if hypochrondriasis were a primary disorder. In the instance of the assassination attempt several injuries were produced which were minor but quite distressing. Loss of equilibrium in particular is extremely disquieting but Hitler was not over-concerned about it (Chapter Three). Indeed, when his mood was normal or elated, Hitler seems to have been characterized more by forbearance of physical distress than by exaggeration of it.

The evidence favouring gallstones is extremely strong and in addition it is likely that direct evidence exists. In 1965 Lev Bezymenski, a Russian historian, published a book describing an autopsy done on a badly burned body found in the garden of the Reich's chancellory just after the battle for Berlin.[1] Russian authorities identified the body as Hitler's and careful comparison of skull and dental X-rays confirm the claim.[2] Hitler's body had been burned by his aides in a gasoline fire and there had been extensive damage,but nevertheless a skilled pathologist could have discovered enormous amounts of information. Bezymenski described the autopsy in considerable detail, but there remain conspicuous exceptions and probable omissions. The liver and every other abdominal organ were described, but the gallbladder was never mentioned. If the gallbladder had been normal it would have been described. If it had been destroyed by fire, that too would have been mentioned in order to be consistent with the practice in the rest of the report. In fact, the gallbladder lies in a position where it is protected by the liver, and it would therefore be odd indeed if it had been completely destroyed since the liver was preserved. Furthermore, Bezymenski describes six additional autopsies (probably Eva Braun, General Krebs, Goebbels, his wife, and two of their six children). Most of the bodies were undamaged by fire, but in only one case, a Goebbels' daughter, was the gallbladder described. There is systematic description of liver, spleen, stomach, kidneys, intestines and urinary bladder: every other abdominal organ. There appears to be only one possible reason for the omission of the gallbladder, which is that the Russians tried to make the reports uniform so that Hitler's would not stand alone. The facts are best explained as a clumsy bureaucratic censorship of the reports before publication which missed one. But if so, what could possibly be the purpose of such falsification? Political motives seem logical for the Russians, like the other Allies, sought to discredit Hitler as a coward, a demon, and a sadist, and they appear to have used the autopsy to that end. There are two other likely examples of political medicine in the autopsy protocol.

The German survivors of the last days unanimously concur that Hitler committed suicide by shooting himself in the head. The autopsy protocol describes head injuries compatible with gunshot or with postmortem injury but then goes on to describe slivers of glass in the mouth and a smell of bitter almonds about the mouth. The Russians concluded that Hitler poisoned himself with cyanide and was possibly shot by an aide after death. Poison was regarded as a cowardly suicide, while to die by gunshot was honorable and manly, points stressed by Bezymenski.[3] Conceivably, slivers of glass in the mouth might have survived the fire, even though the head and oral cavity were virtually destroyed. But potassium cyanide, which gives off the smell of bitter almonds, is quite volatile and could not have persisted through the fire and the eight days of burial. The conclusion must be that the autopsy record is erroneous on this point. The record goes on to say that Hitler was monorchic, that is, he had only one testis. Monorchism is unimportant medically as it would have had no physiological effect at all and no particular psychological problems are associated with the condition. However, from the political viewpoint of the Russians, monorchism might be expected to carry negative implications to discredit Hitler's image as a man and a national leader, and thus there is plausible motive for fraud in their report. Whether the reported finding is true or not cannot be determined; the external genitalia could have been destroyed by fire, as was the abdominal wall, but this is conjectural because of course fire can have capricious results. None of Hitler's doctors mentions monorchism but only Morell and possibly Giesing would have been likely to conduct an examination thorough enough to find out. As for the gallbladder, it is clear that definite anatomic pathology associated with Hitler's well-known abdominal distress would put him into the realm of the common man. But leaving the abdominal complaint vague would heighten the suspicion that Hitler was an emotional casualty. We have tried to obtain copies of the complete autopsy protocol from Russian authorities but without success. In the future when passions have subsided still further, we expect it will be released. Meanwhile, gallstones with associated infection and jaundice is the only plausible diagnosis.

In neuropsychiatric diagnosis, the same analytic procedures are fully applicable but the presentation is complicated because virtually every possible diagnosis and pejorative description in the nomenclature has been applied to Hitler. We will consider in our differential all of the diagnoses that we know to have been seriously suggested.

Amphetamine toxicity is an extremely probable diagnosis, for as we have seen, it can account for Hitler's disorders of emotional control, thinking, and mood described previously. Indeed, Hitler's salient pathological behaviours were consistent with amphetamine abuse in every detail. The fluctuation in signs and the periods of recovery are reasonably explained by changes in dosage and attempts at complete withdrawal of the drug. Amphetamines produce precisely the sort of sleep disturbance which Hitler suffered, and in addition, his depression can be accounted for by the attempts to withdraw the drug. Also, withdrawal is often accompanied by excessive sleeping and eating. None of our informants remembered excessive sleeping, but Hitler occasionally did go on eating binges.[4] Strong evidence is also provided by stereotypic behaviours which are specific signs of severe amphetamine toxicity. Starting in 1940, perhaps even as early as 1938, Hitler began to bite at the skin surrounding the nails of his thumb and the first two fingers on each hand, continuing this habit until near the end.[5] The biting was more intense when he was excited but it was continuous, and Linge described it as 'his most characteristic gesture".[6] The fingertips had a chronically inflamed appearance and they must have been extremely tender, yet he kept on biting. Fastidious, concerned with 'image', but he bit. Such compulsive gnawing is a feature of amphetamine toxicity; indeed rats and our nearer relative, monkeys, will gnaw off their toes, and it is a prominent feature of only one other human illness, an extremely rare disease affecting children.

Then in the middle of 1943, he developed another stereotypic mannerism, the picking at the skin at the back of his neck 'as if he had a double skin . . . as if he wanted to scratch something off'.[7] (These literal translations do not convey the full German meaning: Hitler scratched intensely without any apparent reason.) Another informant used the term '*Juckreitz*' to describe the scratching.[8] *Juckreitz*, a very revealing German word which has no English equivalent, denotes compulsive scratching, being forced to scratch, even though there is nothing visible to cause itching. Picking at the skin and scratching are characteristic of amphetamine toxicity. Abusers may develop deep excoriations and infections as, indeed, Hitler developed infections at the back of his neck (see Appendix A). A few other disorders are associated with intense itching and rarely is it a symptom of psychiatric illness of other kinds, which somewhat compromises its differential value as a sign. Intense itching also is a prominent symptom of jaundice due to the obstruction of bile flow, but because Hitler scratched through years when there was no evident jaundice, this cause is unlikely. The scratching done by amphetamine abusers is often associated with a peculiar delusion, that insects are burrowing under the skin. While Hitler never expressed such beliefs, he may well have had the delusion.

Only two quite minor elements of the complete syndrome associated with amphetamine toxicity are missing: abusers often lose weight while taking the drug and then regain it when they stop. There was little if any fluctuation in Hitler's weight, and Heinz Linge said that he never had his uniforms altered or the size changed.[9] The second missing element was bruxism, the grinding together of teeth in the upper and lower jaw, which is sometimes notable among amphetamine abusers. Our informants did not remember Hitler doing it and it is unlikely that such a mannerism would be forgotten.

This extremely strong evidence of amphetamine toxicity is complemented by other evidence described in Chapter Five, where it was shown that the observed effects of a drug Hitler was receiving were compatible with amphetamine or cocaine and with no other drug. Thus there was surely exposure to an agent capable of producing the signs and symptoms just described. Moreover, as we will proceed to demonstrate, those signs and symptoms are best explained by amphetamine or cocaine toxicity. Two sets of evidence point to one cause of Hitler's behavioural disorder and both sets independently exclude other causes. Short of having actual chemical determination of drug levels in Hitler's blood during a time when he was exhibiting symptoms, stronger evidence could hardly be demanded.

However, a few other diagnostic possibilities do warrant discussion. Heinrich Himmler and others since have suggested central nervous system syphilis.[10] Syphilis is protean in its manifestations, a notorious imitator of other diseases. Hitler did have negative serological tests for syphilis (see Appendix C) which makes neurosyphilis unlikely but does not eliminate it. The critical point in the evidence against a diagnosis of syphilis is that there was no dementia, and in particular, no loss of memory. Dementia invariably occurs in neurosyphilis usually as a first manifestation, but if not initially, it appears within a few months. Also, neurosyphilis usually produces distinctive eye signs. Hitler had a competent examination by Dr Loehlein (see Appendix C) which discovered no abnormalities. Syphilis need not be considered further.

Morell regarded Hitler first as manic-depressive, later as suffering from encephalitis, and finally as having a brain tumour. All persons with behavioural and neurologic disorders must be regarded as brain tumour suspects. The common varieties of brain tumour grow rapidly enough so that a two and a half year illness would be impossible. But there are exceptions, and a tumour cannot be absolutely eliminated on that ground. Personality change is associated with tumours of the frontal lobes of the brain, but the changes reported are unlike those exhibited by Hitler. Moreover, dementia, epileptic seizures, and other signs would be expected to appear. However, a tumour would still have to be considered a remote possibility if it were not for the periods of near recovery. Brain tumours in certain places can produce intermittent signs, but utterly different than those of Hitler, and therefore a diagnosis of tumour would be extremely difficult to defend.

Manic-depressive illness deserves serious consideration. This disease, a common psychiatric disorder, features cyclic swings in mood between extremes of depression and euphoria. Irritability, grandiosity, euphoria, and depression are all hallmarks of manic-depressive illness. Recovery from an episode is typically complete just as Hitler's recoveries were complete or nearly complete. The evidence against manic-depressive illness consists of an accumulation of small technical points, none of which in itself is conclusive but together they greatly weaken the argument for the diagnosis. Hitler's sleep disturbance was definitely *initial insomnia*. He had trouble falling asleep, but once asleep, tended to oversleep in the morning. Manic depressives generally have *terminal insomnia*: when depressed, they fall asleep at ordinary times, but awaken too early in the morning, or exactly opposite to Hitler's pattern. When manic, they feel little need for sleep and often go for extended periods without sleep or with very little sleep. But manics do not usually complain of sleeplessness or fatigue, whereas Hitler did complain. Hitler's thinking became more rigid and he immersed himself in detail. Manics, in contrast, tend strongly to become loose and expansive in their thinking and to become more global and general. Manic-depressive illness is transmitted genetically. This means that Hitler, if manic depressive, would have received the gene or genes from one of his parents and other family members might have been affected. None was. At nearly fifty years of age, he was old for a first attack of mania. Hitler's depressed periods are not well known, probably because they were infrequent and short in addition to the fact he withdrew as much as possible from observation; but his more active periods are better described. Manics may be irritable, extremely so, but there are nevertheless periods when the euphoria, the 'infectious gaiety', of the manic breaks through. Hitler never exhibited that. He liked to be gay and he liked animated parties, but he was not a central figure who would initiate that sort of fun. Finally, manic-depressive illness cannot account for the stereotypic behaviour described above.

Schizophrenia can be dismissed as a diagnosis because of lack of major signs. However, schizophrenia does present a diagnostic problem because some people with a schizophrenic genotype (they have the necessary genes) never develop overt schizophrenia, but they instead exhibit deviations of personality which range from near schizophrenia to near normal. These particular disorders which are called 'schizoid' or 'schizotypy' or 'schizophrenic spectrum' by researchers are today the focus of intense study because they constitute the outstanding unsolved problem in psychiatric classification. Schizotypy is suggested by some of Hitler's premorbid traits, in particular his tendency to overvalue his ideas (and disregard those of others), and some aspects of his premorbid history, for example, his relative social isolation in Vienna where he seems to have had only one close human relationship with August Kubizek which he soon abandoned. Moreover, pre-war and early post-war accounts of Hitler's life, which mainly relied on data tainted by propagandistic purposes, tended to emphasize aspects of his personality even more suggestive of schizotypy. Although the facts have been slowly undergoing correction since these accounts appeared, some evidence supporting an impression of the young Hitler as a feckless eccentric remains.

Unfortunately the questions introduced by the possibility of schizotypy can be addressed only by technical experts who would need a separate book, but in such circumstances, expert opinions may serve in lieu of a full exposition. As it happens, the University of Minnesota has a unique concentration of three internationally recognized experts in the genetics of schizophrenia and the delimitation of the schizoid. Each expert independently answered the question: 'What is your personal probability based on the relevant chapters in this book and all other information you may have that Hitler was a schizotype with 0 = no possibility, 1 = certain schizotype.' The estimates were 0·33, 0·35 and 0·55, or an average of 0·41. The expectancy of schizotypy in the population can be very roughly estimated at 0·04, so the experts have assigned Hitler a substantial added probability. Of course schizotypy, if present, could not account for the main features of Hitler's psychiatric decline, so why is the question worth raising? Well, aside from getting authoritative estimates on record because the question will likely be resurrected from time to time as information about Hitler and about the variability of the schizophrenic genotype becomes better known, there is this simple fact: some schizoids, probably a minority, may be extraordinarily sensitive to amphetamine. At least there is excellent theoretical reason to think so and some factual evidence.[12] If so, small doses would be expected to produce exaggerated toxic effects in behaviour. Thus there is a small but definite probability that Morell and Hitler were dealing with an idiosyncratic response to drugs and this is probably the main practical consideration for history.

Those are the diagnoses that warrant consideration, but Hitler has been called virtually every other name in the psychiatric glossary. None is supportable. He was at least forty-nine years old when his neuropsychiatric illness became manifest, and that alone makes many psychiatric diagnoses extremely unlikely. He had no features of a neurotic illness—no incapacitating anxiety, no compulsions, no obsessions, no phobias. Likewise, there is no evidence remotely suggestive of encephalitis or a post-encephalitic syndrome or any form of diffuse brain disease. Sexual deviations of several kinds have been suggested, but the fact remains that very little is known about Hitler's sex life. Ignorance has fostered blatant speculation. The evidence is: he was regarded as sexually normal by his physicians and by those who knew him through the war. Eva Braun, his mistress, was thought by all to be a thoroughly normal young woman. Hitler was an emotional person who certainly grieved deeply and appropriately following the death by suicide of an earlier mistress, Geli Raubal. Eva Braun voluntarily came to Berlin during the last days, elected to marry

Hitler and then to die with him. Hitler was certainly capable of sustaining for a lengthy period a relationship involving profound affectional ties. Saying more would be sheer speculation.

It has also been assumed that Hitler's deterioration was due to the increasing stress of defeat on a flawed psychopathic personality. There is first of all no evidence of a significant premorbid personality disorder, but that diagnosis, even if it were applicable, is too weakly predictive to be very useful and is not needed anyhow because normal people are quite vulnerable to prolonged stress. The evidence against the theory of stress as a cause is a minor fact—the deterioration began while the war was still going very well for Germany—and a major one—Hitler's signs and symptoms were not those seen in such reactions. Stress reactions feature disabling anxiety and fearfulness; and, if the stress is prolonged and intense, a confusional state may appear. The affected person appears extremely frightened and distraught and the common reaction is to withdraw as permanently as possible from the threatening situation. Hitler was quite the opposite in all those essential respects.

A more recent group of diagnostic efforts is encompassed by the term 'psychohistory'. There is, unfortunately, little content in these writings and vagueness makes rational discussion of such studies difficult. Also, respected historians have paired their names with the most ethereal of the speculations. The basis of the problem is the uncritical acceptance of psychoanalytic methods and the inappropriate use of them. Psychoanalysis enjoyed a vogue, virtually limited to the United States, as the theoretical basis of psychiatry and a major therapeutic tool. That position has been steadily eroded by discoveries in chemistry, physiology, and genetics; by discovery of the laws governing environmental influence on behaviour; and by the failure of analytic treatment in most applications. Yet a limited place for psychoanalysis, probably helping to resolve minor problems in relatively normal people in order to increase their social effectiveness, may remain.

So why is psychoanalysis not applicable to historical analysis? The simple answer is that the interpretations of psychoanalysis, to the extent that they have logical consistency, require verification and that can be supplied only by the person undergoing analysis. For example, one reputable historian has attributed much of Hitler's problematic behaviour to his belief that his grandfather was a Jew.[13] That is an hypothesis which could, in theory, be confirmed only during the extended analytic process by the person involved, in this case Hitler, and it is conceivable that Hitler might become aware of his motivations for antisemitism and acknowledge them. Even this much would have to be accepted as evidence with grave reservations because patients try to please their analysts and may convince themselves that the expected answers are correct and if they do not, analysts come equipped with a postulated psychic device, 'resistance', which may be invoked when the expected answer is not forthcoming. But of course Hitler cannot supply even that equivocal evidence and therefore it is not possible to take seriously these hypotheses and their numerous variants. For example, Hitler's mother was given an ineffective and painful treatment for her breast cancer by a Jewish physician—hence Hitler's antisemitism.[14] Without collaboration by the patient in analysis, one must then fall back on a basic method of medicine and ask what are the base rates. How many mothers were given treatment for cancer by Jewish physicians that was painful and ineffective? Dozens? Thousands? What proportion of their children developed virulent antisemitism? What proportion of antisemites had analogous experiences? Those are facts needed to back any such assertion and, of course, they are not only unavailable, simply posing the questions destroys the hypothesis.

Even extremely conscientious historians have fallen partial victims to the temptation to make 'psychohistory'. For example, John Toland, in an otherwise factually accurate book, quotes Dr Edmund Forster to the effect that Hitler had psychiatric evaluation during his hospitalization for blindness in 1918.[15] Hitler was said to have had hallucinations induced by hypnosis and was diagnosed as a psychopath with hysterical tendencies. In fact, Toland appears to have been desperately reaching for some psychological explanation for Hitler. But the incident as described is medically absurd and, in fact, Robert Waite has severely criticized Toland's handling of it.[16] Forster was quoted from an unreliable account. This misuse of psychiatry should have ended in 1940 when, in response to absurd conjectures about Hitler, Francis Walshe, a leading British neurologist, wrote, 'Hitler is a nasty piece of work and may deserve the bigger and uglier words that psychiatrists use, but does it mean anything?'[17]

The evidence is extremely strong in support of one basic cause for Hitler's psychiatric disability, amphetamine toxicity, and no other diagnosis. Through plausible mechanisms, amphetamine also can account for Hitler's neurological deterioration and his heart disease: otherwise, accounting for these conditions will require one or more additional diagnoses. We begin with the neurological deterioration and quickly find difficulties with the tremor. The physiologic tremor that Hitler exhibited is an exaggeration of the normal oscillation of nervous impulses which maintain muscle tone. It is the tremor which in normal people may make threading a needle difficult. It is commonly increased by emotional arousal, fatigue, and many toxic states, including hangovers and amphetamine toxicity. But one aspect of Hitler's tremor is not easily explained by simple toxicity: the tremor was for six months limited to the left arm and hand before it spread to the left leg and finally the right arm and hand. This progression is not typical of exaggerated physiological tremor which, while often more apparent on one side of the body, is rarely, if ever, so intensely focused in one extremity. We have not heard such a case described or found one in the medical literature. We have also searched for reports of interactions between amphetamine and the other drugs taken by Hitler producing tremor, but none accounts for the evidence. No other type of tremor precisely fits the evidence either, although the *familial tremor* looks much like the physiological tremor. But it is inherited as an autosomal dominant disorder and Hitler's parents were unaffected. Once established, usually in adolescence, it persists through life. Hitler's tremor developed at age forty-nine and was intermittent.

Morell regarded Hitler's tremor as hysterical and, as was true of the abdominal distress, historians have tended to accept that diagnosis. Tremor is seen in hysteria but rarely. When it does

121

occur, it has a bizarre quality, usually consisting of coarse jerking movements, frequent changes in character, and is seen with the other manifestations of hysteria described earlier. Hitler sought to hide his tremor but hysterics display their tremors. Hysteria cannot explain the tremor.

The first of many to attribute the tremor to Parkinson's disease was Professor Maximilian de Crinis, a leading German neurologist who based his opinion on a newsreel, never having personally examined Hitler. The newsreel footage depicting Hitler's movements that we saw was equivocal with respect to muscular rigidity but the tremor was not pictured, although de Crinis may have seen other films. There is, however, strong evidence against Parkinson's disease. It is one of the few disorders which is so distinctive that it is nearly impossible not to notice or to misdiagnose, even for lay observers. None of those for whom we demonstrated a Parkinson's tremor recognized it as Hitler's. All, however, did recognize our demonstration as typical of the disease. Also, the tremor was certainly not a resting tremor as Parkinsonian tremors are, and was most likely increased by purposive movement—an intention tremor. Not one of the six physicians who had close contact with Hitler during his last year mentioned that he even suspected Parkinson's disease and the four who were asked after the war (Morell, Giesing, von Hasselbach, Brandt) specifically rejected the diagnosis. Finally, the period of recovery or near recovery would seem to exclude Parkinson's disease. Once established, the signs of Parkinson's disease persist with little variation.

Having eliminated Parkinson's disease, however, we are embarrassed by the fact that the progression of Hitler's tremor from limb to limb is typical of Parkinson's tremor and no other. Of course, such loose ends are hardly rare in medical practice, but doctors find them perturbing and look for possible, if unproven, explanations. First, we may not have complete information. Tremor is generally reported as an incidental effect of a disease and most case reports of amphetamine toxicity simply note the presence of tremor and do not describe it in detail. Tremor that begins in one extremity and progresses to others may not be unknown despite its absence in our personal experience and our inquiries of other clinicians and the literature. Another possibility is suggested by the fact that known actions of amphetamine involve the same brain chemical (dopamine) that is implicated in Parkinson's disease and prolonged administration of amphetamine is associated with changes in levels of the enzyme needed to produce dopamine. Remembering Hitler's age and the length of time he used drugs (he was older and used them longer than persons in case reports), it is quite reasonable that some Parkinsonian features might result.

So to conclude, if there were another diagnosis that could be supported by the evidence, of course making it would be warranted. Since there is not, the most reasonable explanation, given that the tremor was more like a physiologic tremor exaggerated by toxicity than any other, is that the toxic agent was most likely amphetamine and that the chronic long-term administration perhaps combined with some physiologic eccentricity of Hitler's led to a total syndrome that had Parkinsonian elements.

Two vascular disorders, the stroke (or strokes) in February 1945 and the possible myocardial infarction of 1943, may also be related to amphetamines though, unlike the tremor, alternative explanations are at hand. We have noted that amphetamines, especially when intravenously injected, often produce spasms and functional occlusions of small blood vessels. Hitler's borderline hypertension and his relatively advanced age compared to other amphetamine abusers would likely increase his risk for vascular damage: therefore, there is the possibility that both his brain and likely heart damage were produced by this mechanism. Alternatively, vascular disease unrelated to amphetamine might well have caused the vascular problems. A stroke would be a fairly rare event at Hitler's age, a myocardial infarction would not be so rare, but the combination of the two would be distinctly improbable (unless an infarction initiated a stroke, which is not a rare event, but for which the timing is wrong in Hitler's case). The most parsimonious explanation, given the lack of conclusive evidence, is to attribute both vascular events to the injection of intravenous amphetamine. We should also note that vascular disease can cause tremor, but this mechanism cannot readily explain the variability in Hitler's tremor and especially the period of recovery.

The eye condition which developed in 1945 may or may not be related to amphetamines. Dr Loehlein's examination suggests a vascular event like those associated with amphetamine. Amphetamine causes spasm and sometimes occlusions of retinal vessels. However, competent ophthalmologists have told us that there are no blood vessels that could possibly bleed into the vitreous humour of the eye, giving the precise result described by Dr Loehlein. The nearest alternative diagnostic possibility is vitreous detachment, but no pain is associated with that condition and Hitler did complain of a 'light stabbing pain'. This affliction will have to remain undiagnosed.

His remaining diagnoses are not problematic. All possible diagnoses as they would be listed in a hospital chart are:

ADOLF HITLER

DIAGNOSES

ICD–8*

Number	*Main Diagnoses*
1) 309.1	Non-psychotic organic brain syndrome with amphetamine abuse
2) 304.6	Drug dependence, amphetamine
3) 410.9	Myocardial infarction, probable, secondary to No 1
4) 436.0	Acute but ill-defined cerebrovascular disease, probable, secondary to No 1
5) 574.0	Gallbladder calculus with
6) 575.1	Chronic cholecystitis and
7) 574.102	Choledocholithiasis
8) 503.903	Chronic sinusitis

Other and inactive conditions
Benign vocal cord polyps, status post op.
Ruptured tympanic membranes, bilateral, status post op.
Irritant gas injury to eyes with temporary blindness, no sequela.
Gunshot wound (shrapnel) left thigh, no sequela.

* Eighth Revision International Classification of Diseases, adapted for use in the United States Public Health Service Publication No 1693. USGPO Washington.

CHAPTER EIGHT

Hitler, Medicine and History

A comprehensive description and analysis of the probable re-lationships between Hitler's medical condition and the immense historical events that were part of his life are far beyond the scope of this book. However, we feel well positioned to begin the process with this first overview. It will be the task of historians to refine and further expand the material in this chapter.

Any medical statement about the likelihood of events is based largely on accumulated knowledge of what has happened to groups of persons having the same illness or subjected to the same treatments. Hitler's most problematic disorder was apparently caused by amphetamine toxicity, a common condition for which there are many published cases for comparison; however, we must be mindful of several caveats. While there exist many hundreds of case reports to guide us, none exactly duplicates the case of Adolf Hitler. In particular, his age sets him apart in comparison to others who used amphetamine. Also, he was taking other drugs which affected behaviour; while many of those whose case reports appear in the medical literature were also taking numerous drugs, the confounding drugs were not the same. Moreover, drugs affect-ing behaviour interact in complex ways with social environment as well as the personality of the user. Any account of events involving Hitler will be imperfect but it will be much more accu-rate history if medical evidence is included.

As we have seen, his first illness brought him episodic visceral pain. The pain itself would have been debilitating when present: visceral pain is accompanied by intense feelings of nausea and prostrating weakness which invariably lead to withdrawal and inattention to the external environment. The 'I-don't-care-if-I-die' feeling associated with nausea and vomiting is a good approximation familiar to most. During such an episode, Hitler could not have made fully rational decisions; however, attacks of pain were relatively infrequent, most of them were brief, and therefore his periods of incapacity were probably short. We know of only one convincing example, described by Irving, of an attack of biliary colic actually influencing the course of events.[1] This occurred during the August 1941 episode of illness described in Chapter One. Because of his weakness, fever and pain, Hitler could not follow events closely enough to ensure that his overall strategic plan for the capture of Moscow was executed and his generals covertly substituted a different plan favoured by them. According to Irving, Hitler's plan may have offered the better chances for success. At least this episode warrants detailed attention from military historians.

Pain also has psychological consequences and Hitler himself (p. 22) and many of his followers have suggested that the pain caused him to 'accelerate his plans'. However, if this was his intention, it is hard to explain why his projected dates of action generally lagged the actual pace of events. For example, he projected that the war which came in 1939 would begin around 1943. Hitler may have thought that he was speeding events, but, once set in motion, they as likely obeyed a fatal momentum of their own.

The second illness is attributable to amphetamines and before considering the likely influence of that drug on history, an estimate of when Hitler actually began taking it is needed. The evidence on this crucial point is sketchy, but we will present what we have found and offer an interpretation based upon those findings.

Definite toxicity can, as described, be dated from the late summer of 1942. But intermittent use of amphetamine in low doses could have begun at any time after 1936 when the drug first became available. Indeed, the first hints of possible change in personality similar to those associated with amphetamine usage appeared in late 1937. Sir Neville Henderson, the British Ambassador in Berlin, described Hitler's 'isolation and rages, his loss of faith in the fidelity of his followers' which Henderson regarded as a 'change in his entire outlook on life'.[2] Albert Speer also described a change at about that time. Before 1937, Speer states that Hitler was relaxed, friendly, and accessible; after that, however, he became more withdrawn. According to Speer, 'The genial relaxed Hitler whom I had known in the early thirties had become even to his intimate entourage a forbidding despot with few human relationships.'[3] In 1938 Heinrich Himmler, who had begun compiling a medical file on Hitler, told his confidant Felix Kersten that Hitler had definite mental signs of neurosyphilis.[4] Count Ciano, the Italian Foreign Minister, wrote in his diary on 7 May 1938 that it had been suggested by Victor Emanuel III, the King of Italy, that Hitler was having himself injected with stimulants and narcotics.[5] Narcotics were in fact being injected at the time for the abdominal pain, and while Victor Emanuel's other remarks about Hitler were regarded by Ciano as possibly only amounting to petty gossip, the mention of stimulants even in that context seems an unlikely invention.

There are also medical observations which suggest amphetamine use in the late 1930s. Linge remembers intermittent biting of the fingertips beginning early in 1939.[6] While few single signs in medicine provide conclusive evidence, this particular practice would have been so foreign to Hitler's impeccable standards of dress and bearing and would, moreover, be known by him to be severely detrimental to his image—nailbiting, close to what Hitler did, was particularly condemned in Germany—that it is difficult to explain without amphetamines. Still other evidence stems from an incident during the negotiations in March 1939 between Hitler and Emil Hacha, President of Czechoslovakia. The political situation in Czechoslovakia was unstable and Hacha travelled from Prague to Berlin for a conference and was informed by Hitler at 1 a.m. that Czechoslovakia would be invaded five hours later unless Hacha surrendered his country. At one delicate point, Hacha physically collapsed: the cause is unclear, but most likely Hacha, who suffered from heart disease and had been awake for eighteen hours, was overcome by physical exhaustion coupled with sustained emotional arousal. Whatever its cause, by the time of Hacha's collapse it was already clear that he would surrender, but Hitler needed Hacha's signature to legalize the event. Although it was by then past 2 a.m., Morell was called to revive him. The essence of what occurred was recorded by several observers[7], but there is a clear eye-witness account, from the ubiquitous Heinrich Hoffmann.[8] Hacha was seated in an armchair with his head back, conscious but breathing heavily. Morell gave him an intravenous injection and 'very quickly' Hacha became 'fresh, alert' and obviously ready to continue. Later Hitler jokingly complained that Hacha had become 'too lively' and Hitler 'was afraid he might not sign'. Significantly, Hacha asked for another injection that night and from that time on he became a patient of Morell's. Evidently the injected drug was powerfully reinforcing. Morell claimed he had only injected vitamins, but no vitamin preparation could produce such a dramatic result. Of the stimulants then in use, only amphetamine or cocaine would produce exactly the result described.

However, since this was only one instance, non-pharmacologic effects combined with another drug must be considered as possibilities, as, for example, even the mild pain of the injection might have produced physiological arousal; an unlikely but remotely possible explanation. The evidence is not conclusive, but it does suggest that Morell had intravenous amphetamine at hand. He is unlikely to have had it available for use as a stimulant in a medical or surgical emergency because the drug was not then (or later) used for such purposes. He would have had it for only one probable reason—to produce immediate arousal.

The Hacha episode introduces other evidence to consider in Hitler's case, for there seems to have been no rational warrant for the invasion of Czechoslovakia. During the previous year the state had been dismembered as part of the infamous Munich accords. Hitler had been officially ceded the Sudeten territories but of course Germany dominated the remnant both politically and economically. Hitler appears to have decided on his course of action within days of Hacha's climactic visit with the evidence pointing towards a hasty and impulsive response to momentary opportunity provided by tensions between the Czech and Slovak populations of the country. This episode marks a change consistent with amphetamine use as well as an important historical milestone. By his senseless annexation, Hitler broke the agreement reached at Munich with Britain's Prime Minister, Neville Chamberlain, and ensured that further rectification of the Treaty of Versailles would be resisted with force.[9] Immediately following the Hacha episode, Great Britain unilaterally guaranteed Poland's borders. With this particular aggression, world opinion changed and congealed, with Hitler becoming definitely known as an international outlaw.

Although the Hacha episode is a convenient marker, in fact Hitler's behaviour in diplomatic conferences had changed at least a year before that. After assuming power in 1933, he had been mannerly and controlled, though firm. Men such as Anthony Eden and Lloyd George, a future and a past Prime Minister of Britain, were favourably impressed by Hitler. Eden described Hitler as 'smart, elegant, controlled, quick-witted and knew the subject being discussed'. Lloyd George, too, had praised Hitler as 'the George Washington of Germany, a man of supreme quality'. These are not exceptional statements. But starting in 1938 there came the famous series of diplomatic confrontations during which Hitler berated, bullied, and issued ultimatums: here was born the stereotype which the rest of the world came to fear. The conventional explanation of the change is that Hitler was merely acting or feigning rages in order to bully and intimidate his diplomatic opponents. Perhaps this is so, but this interpretation credits Hitler with immense acting skills and the ability to foresee the success of such behaviour against men widely experienced in life and European power politics. Alternatively, amphetamines could explain the change in Hitler's behaviour, or, more likely, could have been acting in combination with Hitler's growing confidence in German power and intoxication with his own successes. Amphetamine increases aggressiveness and risk-taking: those particular elements in Hitler's personality became highly exaggerated.

Given the evidence as described, it is most likely that the course of events occurred as follows. By 1937 Hitler became well acquainted with amphetamine through newspapers and probably official military reports. These reports were highly favourable, even laudatory, and Hitler certainly talked to Morell about the new 'miracle' drug. During one crisis or another, Hitler, already a user of drugs to modify his physiology, probably wanted to try amphetamine to increase his confidence and stamina and Morell, though more cautious, co-operated. Hitler would have then experienced the euphoria, the increases in confidence, stamina, and apparent mental efficiency produced by amphetamine. Moreover, the crises were successively resolved with results more favourable for Hitler than he had probably believed possible. Accordingly, the pattern was set. If Hitler followed a typical pattern of progressive drug use, at first low dose oral preparations would have been used, and then only intermittently. But as crises became more frequent with an escalating intensity, amphetamine became a routine part of the preparation for antici-pated stress.

If this scenario is close to what actually happened, as we think it was, it leads to the further question: could the use of amphetamine by one man have contributed importantly to starting World War II? This question will require extensive new study of the historical sources by specialized experts but at this point the conclusion must be that amphetamines had at most a small role. Europe was unstable with or without Hitler. Moreover, Hitler's policy, indeed a cornerstone of his whole political philosophy, was expansion of Germany to the east. Those aims were widely known long before amphetamine could have influenced his behaviour. He did not want war with the Western powers, but he had long planned a Russian war. While few politicians once in power do what they had planned (or promised), we think it is impossible not to credit Hitler with the intention and the capability of making war. In addition, geopolitical realities almost guaranteed that the Western nations would become involved because Hitler could not get land access to Russia without violating the sovereignty of states to which France or England or both owed binding treaty obligations. However, drugs may well have influenced the specific starting date and place of the war which resulted. In fact we think that the primary effect of amphetamine would have been to increase the probability of early success for Hitler. The international political environment up to the Hacha episode happened to favour boldness, confidence, and bluff. Deliberateness, restraint, or vacillation, all qualities Hitler had previously exhibited, might well have delayed the implementation of Hitler's plans and might even have defeated them. But Hitler would not have given them up short of defeat. Most likely defeat would have come to Hitler in any event, but without amphetamine, it could have come much earlier.

For the first two years of the war Hitler's leadership was masterly. He proved himself innovative, flexible, and supremely competent. If he was taking amphetamine, its use probably remained occasional and no major signs of toxicity developed. Through this period the increased boldness, self-confidence, and optimism associated with amphetamine use were consistent with Hitler's behaviour, but those were heady days for him anyhow. Drugs would hardly be needed to elevate mood. Nor was there particular need to prepare for personal confrontations: who could raise issue with him? Although Hitler may well have taken amphetamine from time to time, there is no hint of adverse effects.

A period of crisis and change occurred through the winter of 1941–2, during the battles near Moscow. German armies barely missed capturing the city before exhaustion and the extreme Russian winter stopped them. Inadequately prepared for a winter war and subjected to strong Russian attacks mounted by fresh troops, the German army came near to collapse and rout. Memories of Napoleon's disaster at Moscow haunted the German commanders, who wanted to retreat. But Hitler, fearing that a retreat once begun could not be stopped, forbade it and ordered front-line troops to stand fast. The military crisis bordered on catastrophe for nearly three months. But the line held.

This period of the 'winter war' is medically ambiguous. Here for the first time there appeared possible new signs of drug toxicity: rigidity of thinking manifest by the 'no retreat' policy, increased irritability, the first instances of sticking on minor details, and projection of blame on to others. Field Marshal Keitel, who was in daily contact with Hitler through this period, gives several examples in his book,[10] for example: 'Early in December the drive for Tikhvin in the north, which the Führer had tactically launched against the War Office's advice, but which already contained in it the seeds of failure, suffered a reverse.' The commander, a field marshal, asked 'for freedom of action and to be permitted to withdraw part of his front . . . in good time in order to shorten his front'. Permission was denied by Hitler and the commander's resignation was accepted. Hitler, said Keitel about this and another very similar case, 'sacrificed two first-class commanders only to provide scapegoats for the first setbacks; he had no desire to recognize that he himself was actually to blame'. Projection of blame for personal mistakes was a new element in Hitler's personality. He previously had held acceptance of responsibility to be a major test of character and several times had acknowledged embarrassing errors, for example, the failure of the 'beer hall *Putsch*'. Keitel also described excessive irritability manifest, for example, when Hitler learned that one of his commanders had made an unauthorized retreat. Keitel said:[11]

> The Führer flew into an uncontrolled temper, and ordained Hoepner's [the general at fault] immediate removal from the army command. . . . The Führer fulminated all night long in our reading room cursing at his generals who had not been brought up to obey.

Hitler may have been correct in his action, but it is the excessive time and emotional energy spent in 'fulmination' that arouses suspicion of drug use. The suspicion increases because a few days later another general was dismissed for exactly the same reason and Keitel remarked that Hitler remained 'absolutely composed'. Behaviour is relatively predictable in that it tends strongly to repeat. When explaining such great differences in the response to similar situations arising closely together in time, some major difference in environment must be sought. Amphetamine could have been that difference if it were present on the first occasion and absent or present in lower amount on the second. Alternative explanations are not apparent. About this time, Hitler took two other decisive steps. He assumed personal command of the army which was consistent with pathological grandiosity induced by amphetamine and mistrust (of his generals). And, immediately following the Japanese attack on Pearl Harbor on 7 December 1941, he declared war against the United States. For a year there had been a *de facto* naval war in the Atlantic initiated by the United States, but Hitler was under no binding obligation to make the war formal. He acted against the advice of his foreign office but again consistently with grandiosity, impulsivity, and poor judgement, for which he paid dearly. For if Hitler had bided his time, President Roosevelt would have had great difficulty in entering the European War and the focus of American efforts would have been in the Pacific.

There are also points to be made against amphetamine use in 1941–2. Through this period Germany experienced her first significant military reversal and there was deep division between Hitler and some military commanders. Thus there was understandable strain on Hitler and cause for acrimony. Moreover, it is now generally agreed that Hitler's policy of standing fast did in fact save the army and that it was the only military decision that could have done so. A more detailed look at Hitler's military decisions as we understand them does suggest considerably more flexibility and innovation than would be possible given severe amphetamine toxicity. We conclude that Hitler most likely increased his use of amphetamine probably because he sought the increase in stamina and optimism, and at times he was significantly impaired by unwanted toxic effects such as grandiosity, impulsiveness, and irritability. However, the toxic signs did not persist for extended periods.

In the middle of 1941 the decisions were made which led to the mass extermination of Jews, gypsies, and Russian prisoners. There is no record of the deliberations that led to establishment of the death camps. Earlier there had been sporadic and vague discussions of deporting Jews to Madagascar, which slowed and eventually ceased, but which were not replaced. Hitler, of course, would have had to know about the 'final solution' and most likely originated it. However, the noted historian David Irving has recently disputed those assumptions.[12] Because there is no record, however, we cannot make reasonable inferences about Hitler's mental status, and, therefore, we can have no strong opinion about the effect of amphetamine on the outcome. We can make the general point that the decision to establish the death camps with all the far-reaching logistical complications thereby implied, and to do mass murder, certainly required long-range planning and perspective. Pathological decisions due to amphetamine are, in contrast, likely to be those made impulsively in response to more immediate stimuli. Moreover, even if Hitler had made an off-hand, impulsive decision to carry out the final solution, that decision would have taken time even to begin to implement. Hitler at worst was not always in a toxic state from amphetamine and, if he had ever regretted an impulsive decision, he certainly had plenty of opportunity to reverse it while maintaining secrecy. We incline towards the view of Eberhard Jäckel: Hitler, realizing after the failure of the German attempt to capture Moscow that the war would be long, and that total victory was unlikely, carried out the most extreme implication of the Nazi programmes.[13]

The battle of Stalingrad and subsequent events were almost certainly influenced by amphetamine toxicity. We have described the early signs of Hitler's illness beginning about the time the Stalingrad disaster took form. The 'no retreat' policy was now applied irrationally in the light of the strategic situation and it was sustained by unrealistically optimistic estimates of the future course of events. Unlike the situation at Moscow, the Sixth Army at Stalingrad was about to be surrounded. Hitler's military commanders repeatedly pointed out the extreme danger of the situation, had planned the withdrawal of the 300,000 soldiers, and begged him to issue the necessary orders. Hitler had, however, committed his prestige to the retention of his foothold on the Volga. This in itself included a new element of grandiosity: before, Hitler had been more tentative, taking chances to be sure but worrying about the possible outcomes, and, where feasible, leaving himself a way out. Now there appeared an unreasoning optimism which Hitler supported argumentatively by any reason at hand, no matter how flimsy. For example, Göring guaranteed to supply the Sixth Army by air. His arithmetic was immediately challenged on irrefutable grounds, but Hitler seized upon Göring's statements and refused to listen to other estimates. Even after the extremely poor performance of the first few days of the airlift, Hitler persisted in his optimism and hope. Indeed, his unreasoning optimism dominated the next weeks until finally the army was lost: about 6,000 men returned to Germany after the war. (Typhus killed many of the men taken prisoner.)

The contribution of Hitler's mental rigidity and overly optimistic view to the tragedy of Stalingrad could be more richly illustrated, but for medical purposes, the almost simultaneous disaster at El Alamein provides simpler contrasts. Hitler had enjoyed following the war in North Africa, which had swept back and forth over great reaches of desert. One of Field Marshal Rommel's most effective tactics was the fighting retreat and counter-attack, and Rommel was one of Hitler's favourites. But in November 1942, when the great El Alamein battle was being fought and Rommel wanted flexibility of action, Hitler instructed that 'every yard of ground must be held—no retreat'. His communication to Rommel contained an early example of the repetitive slogans that began to replace innovative thought: 'Stronger will triumphant over stronger battalions . . . Victory or Death'.

From that time onward, Hitler largely lost the flexibility and innovation that had marked his earlier military thinking. Again and again the slogan 'no retreat' and Hitler's rigid unyielding insistence on this single alternative became the cornerstone of German strategy despite begging and pleas from his military commanders and the catastrophes that followed. His everlasting concern with details made even local adjustments of the front lines difficult. To be sure retreats were made and were often handled masterfully by Hitler and his generals but most came after the optimal moment.

His decisions concerning weapons research were at least as detrimental as his direct management of armies. We have described the earlier Hitler as extraordinarily able to grasp concepts, weigh alternatives with all of their practical and theoretical nuances, and come out with clear rationally defensible courses of action. He was well aware that technological advances could rapidly date weapons systems, and early in the war he strongly advocated basic research and weapons development. But after 1941, he failed, despite repeated opportunities, to grasp the importance of jet aeroplanes, atomic energy, heat-seeking rockets, sound-seeking torpedoes, ground-to-air-missiles, and radar. All of these decisive technological advances were well within the grasp of German research and development but all were aborted or delayed by Hitler's neglect or interference. For example, Germany developed the first jet fighters, but their production was delayed by many months because Hitler insisted that they be equipped as bombers, thereby introducing insurmountable problems in design.[14] When the aeroplanes did finally arrive, they were extremely effective against the British and American bombing offensive. If they had arrived earlier they might well have defeated the Allies in the air. But at the time even the development of the jet bombers was an unwelcome diversion to Hitler, who basically was clinging tenaciously to a single alternative weapons system, long-range rockets, and he did so long after it was clear that rockets were too limited in payload and accuracy to play any significant role. His rigidity effectively froze German research into a few limited areas and in those areas Hitler often interfered with disastrous effect. Amphetamines did not lose the war for Germany, but we think their contribution to the cause of the Allies had some significance.

By the late summer of 1942, Hitler seemed to be in a more or less chronic toxic state. A few months later, just after the defeat at Stalingrad, he was evidently extremely depressed and of course the defeat alone could have been cause enough for depression. However, as will be seen, it was also a logical time to withdraw amphetamine, and that, too, produces severe depression. In fact the terrible fate of the Stalingrad army had been sealed at least a month before the depression began, a month during which Hitler was as optimistic and expansive as ever. That month requires explanation because depression in reaction to a depressing event generally comes immediately after the event; but in Hitler's case, during the intervening month the southern front in Russia had to be patched together and we think amphetamines were continually administered, thus delaying the onset of the depression.

Eventually the front was stabilized, the war slowed down, and Hitler and Morell could no longer avoid facing the malign entanglement they had created. Yet during the winter of 1943, what the two men knew or guessed about the true nature and extent of their problem is uncertain. The literature of medicine held no guides, for Hitler may well have been receiving amphetamines through an unprecedented period of time and in unprecedented amounts: he was himself an experimental animal. We can, however, make some reasonable surmises regarding Hitler's and Morell's perspective of the problem. Detrimental changes in mental state, to the extent they were noted by Hitler or Morell and associated with amphetamine, would have been recognized at that time as reversible and hence of only passing importance. Besides, the subjective benefits no doubt still appeared to Hitler large by comparison with any of the untoward effects. Morell, though perhaps not Hitler, would have had to note increasing tolerance which would have been worrisome and which might have pressed him towards a decision to withdraw the drug. But the critical effect that moved the two men to action was most likely the effects of amphetamine on Hitler's heart. By this time the first of Dr Weber's alarming electrocardiogram reports had been received and there is an unmistakable association between intravenous amphetamine and stress on the heart. An injection produces an immediate increase in heart rate and strength of contraction which is experienced as rapid pounding lasting a few seconds, called 'flutter' by abusers. The flutter is always present and if blood supply to the heart muscle is compromised by constriction of arteries there will be pain known as angina pectoris, a second cardiac symptom reported by many amphetamine users. So Hitler surely thought that amphetamine was affecting his heart and may well have experienced angina. Indeed, his age and the fact that some heart damage did occur make angina a likely bet. And, of course, the awareness of this danger to the heart explains Morell's use of digitalis and cardiac stimulants as well as the frequent electrocardiograms. Forced to improvise by his bizarre and extremely difficult medical problem, Morell developed this prophylactic regimen. But withdrawal of amphetamine was the only possible way to eliminate the danger and when the war slackened about February 1943, withdrawal was probably tried but failed. Hitler became depressed and did not recover until April.

During the depression, the military conferences were kept brief and Hitler virtually disappeared. We have noted that Morell diagnosed depression and tried to find a treatment, but failed. Hitler would certainly have associated the missing euphoria and confidence with withdrawal of amphetamine because the effects of the drug are so obvious and immediate. Still believing himself indispensable to Germany, he resumed taking the drug. Hitler, of course, remained functional: he was not so ill that his incapacity was obvious to those who saw him daily, but it was starkly evident to those who saw him occasionally or rarely. He also had, as described, his good and bad hours as he progressively learned to maintain an equilibrium that maximized optimism and confidence and minimized over-arousal—a difficult balance, but one possible to approximate for brief periods. To achieve this he had an intravenous injection to get started for the day, and then throughout the day he treated himself with oral drug. As the war situation deteriorated, he began to get intravenous injections through the day, maintaining his fragile equilibrium by using the drug to counter the effect of bad news on his mood. At night he had his barbiturates for sleep. The use of 'uppers' for arousal and 'downers' for sleep is a typical pattern of drug abuse that we have seen several times in medical practice and which was discovered independently by many thousands of abusers who followed Hitler. The use of sedatives in dosages sufficient to assure at least some sleep each night appears to give some protection against progression to the most severe degrees of toxicity as, in Hitler's case, he most likely never developed a full psychotic syndrome with flagrant delusions and hallucinations. However, he and his cause did pay a price for his forced sleep. Hitler, once asleep, was unwilling to be awakened in the morning and for this reason, German armies could not react immediately to the D-Day invasion of France.

Abusers rarely take too little drug because if they do, they are depressed. Therefore, Hitler would have usually had an optimal or slightly high dose and would have appeared affable, assured, and in full command. If he had too much drug he would have appeared irritable, mentally stilted, and suspicious. In both states he would have been garrulous, impulsive, and when challenged with intellectually difficult material, mentally rigid and sluggish. This is extremely close to the Hitler which observers have described. For example, Speer speaking of Hitler in 1943 comments: 'Occasionally Hitler still made decisions alertly and spontaneously as he had in the past, and once in a long while he would even listen attentively to opposing arguments. But those times had become so unusual that we afterward made special note of them.'[15]

In May 1943 the second alarming electrocardiographic report was received and during that summer actual heart damage probably occurred. By then Morell knew that amphetamine was producing major problems. We did not find in his records any of the few articles then in print describing amphetamine intoxication. He did, though, receive a letter from an old friend and ex-patient who wondered whether taking amphetamine was advisable in order to give him the endurance needed to negotiate a steep hill on his way back and forth to town.[16] Morell's answer was unequivocal: he advised against amphetamine, describing it as 'a whip for the horse, not fodder'.[17] In the same letter, Morell made what seems to have been an emotional slip. The patient had, in a separate paragraph in different context, enquired about obtaining Vitamultin. Morell answered most emphatically but inappropriately that Vitamultin contained no other ingredients. Morell sounded defensive and guilt-ridden. So it is likely that Morell knew part of what amphetamine could do to his patient, guessed much of the rest, and unable to cope with his medical problem or to take a firm stand with Hitler but afraid for his wealth, even his life, he continued on. Hitler, the indispensable man, his judgement clouded and his thinking impaired but his mood euphoric, probably believed what he often enough said—that he was giving his life to his country.

Few questions about the possible effect of amphetamine on Hitler's military decision are posed by the period 1943–5 because, after Stalingrad and El Alamein, the initiative in the war passed to the Allies and Hitler's contribution to events was largely to react. Germany had in fact lost the war by this time so that probably the most important single question is whether Hitler's incapacity prolonged the war or not. It appears that the Russians did offer peace feelers and that Germany's eastern war might have been settled as only the United States was resolutely committed to 'unconditional surrender'. Hitler, however, believed that premature surrender had undone Germany in World War I but it is also possible, as many have suggested, that he prolonged the war so that the death camps could continue to operate. Historians will have to answer such questions, but we must point out that they are confounded because Hitler's mood could have been almost always abnormal because of drugs. Neither euphoria nor depression facilitates delicate negotiations. Also, his thinking was impaired so that the intellectually difficult task of comprehending Germany's total situation *vis-à-vis* the Allies was surely lacking in depth and original elements. And most important, the negotiations would have been fairly lengthy and required sustained effort from a secure base. After the battle of Stalingrad (at the latest), Hitler probably never had an extended period with the needed stability of mood and thinking: with the next injection he would have been likely to change the basis of any negotiation.

The next major change occurred after the assassination attempt of 20 July 1944. The use of amphetamine was probably stopped because of a combination of factors. Although Hitler was not seriously wounded, his ear injuries produced dramatic symptoms which were reason enough for caution. Also, other doctors became involved in Hitler's treatment and the SS was snooping around suspicious of poisons. Whatever the reason or combination of reasons, amphetamine evidently was stopped because shortly thereafter the tremor greatly improved and his thinking probably improved. Also, during this period Hitler began planning his last strategic initiative, the Ardennes offensive of December 1944. Although the offensive was unsuccessful, the concept was strategically sound and the early planning had some of the old Hitler verve. But the price again was severe depression and by early September the improvement was reversed, surely because amphetamine was again administered. Then on 27 September jaundice was discovered. Again the questionable treatments were stopped and Hitler's mental state definitely cleared dramatically. This time no depression was noted: one may well have occurred but because of jaundice, Hitler was largely isolated through the period when it would have been most intense.

Probably within a few weeks amphetamine was resumed and again an equilibrium was restored, which persisted until February 1945 when Hitler suffered at least one small stroke; but he may well have had several, and, indeed, his rapid decline from this time onward suggests widespread vascular disease. When signs of brain damage developed, again amphetamine was stopped and again a brief depression developed. This was also the time that the obscure eye disorder described earlier (Chapter Three) appeared and that, too, might have influenced the decision to stop the drug.

By now the hour for Adolf Hitler was very late. The effects of brain damage were evident in his movements. His war was lost and with it his political movement. The main result of his life was a towering victory for forces and peoples he despised. Finally, driven deep underground by his enemies, he killed himself by gunshot.

His end by suicide seems ordained. Hitler as prisoner or fugitive is hard to imagine. But amphetamine may well have influenced the time of the ending. There had been plans to continue the war from south Germany if Berlin were lost, and on 20 April, Hitler's birthday, Göring and most of the administrative staff of government had left to prepare the way. Then on 21 April the first Russian artillery was heard: war had come to Hitler. The following day, at the military conference, Hitler, in a depressive rage, despairing and accusing, said that the war was ended and that he would stay in Berlin. He examined his options and planned his death by suicide. He could not, he reasoned, die fighting as a soldier in the streets of Berlin because he might be wounded and fall alive into Russian hands, and his body must be destroyed because otherwise it would be exhibited in a Russian wax museum. Morell, his colluder, offered Hitler an injection of narcotic to calm him down and, after Hitler refused, fled that day with his injections. But of course, Hitler surely knew by then about the depression that came with withdrawal of amphetamine and allowing Morell to leave could have been part of his preparation for the end. If so, even that was partly undone by drugs. Linge was charged with administering eyedrops since Dr Loehlein's visit because, Linge explained, 'he only trusted me, my hand was steady'.[18] Linge also kept Hitler's appointment pad and on it he recorded his administration of the drops—16 April, one drop, 17–19 April, two to three drops daily, 20 April, five drops.[19] Then the dosage increased. During the last week of Hitler's life, through the last entry on 28 April, the dose went from six drops, given three times daily, to thirteen drops. The active ingredient in the eye drops was cocaine.[20]

Afterword

Adolf Hitler may have been a chance aberration so improbable that his like will never recur. While this is a comforting thought, some facets of Hitler's personality and his career fit all too snugly into niches developed by the current political organization of western industrial democracies. Such hints must not be ignored because while the probability of another phenomenon like Hitler is very low, the stakes wagered on the performance of political leaders today are infinite. For if Hitler had had thermonuclear weapons mounted on missiles that could reach anywhere on earth, can anyone doubt that he would have used them?

The health of political leaders has received some attention in medical history,[1] but this largely excludes the main ground of overlap between Hitler and other leaders, the effect of illness on thinking and behaviour. There is a clear parallel between Hitler and Anthony Eden, who is quoted as saying that during the brief 1956 war over the Suez Canal, when Prime Minister he was 'living on benzedrine'.[2] Coincidentally, he also had an attack of biliary colic at the peak of the crisis. But Eden is only one of a long list of world leaders from the nuclear age who were to some degree incapacitated by illness or by needed or unneeded medical treatment. John Kennedy took steroid hormones which often have major and unpredictable effects on thinking and mood. Franklin Roosevelt, during his last year in office, was clearly incapacitated by hypertensive cerebral vascular disease.[3] So, it would appear, was Joseph Stalin, but for a longer time and with the addition of an associated paranoid condition.[4] Winston Churchill, while still Prime Minister, suffered intellectual decline apparently due to cerebral vascular disease and, to judge from his descriptions of his medications, may well have received small doses of stimulant drugs.[5]

In 1965, in an attempt to respond to the problem, the US Congress passed the 25th amendment to the US Constitution which provides for transfer of power if a president becomes medically incapacitated. This was certainly a correct step and it is hard to see how the law could be improved without introducing danger of usurpation of presidential powers, but as we understand its provisions it would be at best extremely difficult to remove a president who was incapacitated in the same way that Hitler was incapacitated. During war it would probably be impossible.

Some insight into the difficulty of removing a leader from office may be found by asking why the Germans did not move effectively against Hitler. That he was at least intermittently incapacitated mentally and emotionally was clear to those exposed to him. And, ironically, his medical problems were all treatable. Why was effective action not taken against him? For one reason, his incapacity followed years of extremely successful leadership. If he had died or retired before the outbreak of the war he would now be remembered as one of the great German leaders. At his highest point, just after the defeat of France, he was adulated and if his policy of seeking peace with Great Britain had succeeded he would have ranked ahead of Bismarck in German history. Only then the turning, one of the most dramatic in history, that led to deaths in the tens of millions. One generalization seems warranted. Once a leader is confirmed by legalizing ceremonies and has a period of success, then no matter how disastrous or ineffective his leadership becomes, unseating him is extremely difficult. In conditions of modern societies, enough of us remain loyal far too long. One special aspect of this misplaced loyalty can be seen in the assassination attempts against Hitler. Up to the war, Hitler was the occasional target of the random attempts by misfits, eccentrics, and madmen that threaten every leader. His escapes were due to random luck. Then, during the war, he lived in military headquarters and was vulnerable only to those around him. As his incompetence became evident and the eventual disaster became more certain, assassination plots and attempts were mounted. And the most distinguishing feature of all those plots and attempts is that they were bungled. Brave men who willingly put their lives on the line in war agonized too long and did not proceed with sufficient resolution. We suggest that this was because they were members of the social establishment whose deepest impulses, shared with their whole social set, were towards sustaining leadership. Being what they were, their radical attempts to solve their problem were enfeebled and unsuccessful. Even in less extreme situations, the same set of inhibitions and impulses that sustain the social order may be nearly insurmountable even when, by any rational analysis, they are inappropriate.

Another set of problems was pointed out in Albert Speer's analysis of the failure to act against Hitler.[6] Speer, who had considered assassinating Hitler and had even made a desperate plan, points out that Hitler was one of the first leaders of a modern technological state. Because of the very nature of technology, power in a modern state focuses on a single point and would do so even if there were no disposition to assume that power, a development we have seen in the United States. The same technology makes possible instant communication so that today the head of a modern state can issue direct orders to individuals anywhere on earth and nearby space. A few decades ago a national leader had no direct control over those executing his directives; his power decreased geometrically with distance. And before aeroplanes and rockets and nuclear weapons, his power was miniscule anyhow, and could only be applied after long delays during which there was plenty of time for modification. A mad George III was limited in the mischief he could cause. A mad Hitler killed 35 million people.

We have so often told ourselves that Hitler could only have arisen in defeated, dispirited Germany that some historical facts that do not wholly support that conclusion should be underscored. We should note for example that in several ways Hitler was a thoroughly modern politician. He was an innovator and a professional. His early political campaigns were much like those waged in western industrial democracies today as Hitler barnstormed about Germany in his private aeroplane making the same basic speech several times each day. He made extensive use of radio, built up local organizations, and put together voting blocks. He originated some of these techniques, polished them all until they worked effectively, and then used them in a quick succession of elections all too reminiscent of American primary campaigns. His monstrous side was not exposed by democratic electoral hurdles. Hitler passed. And while many of his early followers were eccentrics, it was the middle class that he slowly won and that finally gave him an electoral plurality. Of course, we had understood intellectually that during his rise to power, Hitler had won the unquestioning allegiance, even the devotion, of extremely intelligent, principled, and strong-minded men and women. Yet we found it emotionally disquieting to meet, while doing this research, many Germans who had eagerly followed Hitler. They were from all walks of life. Most were alert, intelligent, devoted to their families, doing useful work, and not arrogant or overbearing. Nearly all had good humour, a couple were eccentric, all save one were straightforward. They could have been our neighbours and they had marched with Hitler. We think few of us can be sure that we would have stayed behind.

Another of Hitler's innovations is certainly relevant to modern politics. He was the first prominent example of the professional politician who has since become dominant in western societies. He had no profession and no other source of income. While in his twenties he had decided to make politics his life work. Previously, most political leaders had been drawn from the landed aristocracy or from among successful workers in the trades or professions. Such persons did not need jobs and political office was not a career, it was rather a complement for a successful life, or at worst, a legacy of birth. The rise of the professional politician is a major change in politics and serious questions are posed by it. For there must be some special qualities that would permit one to voluntarily pay the price of a career as a politician: periods of hectic speechmaking; public scrutiny on demand; constant guard against chance remarks that could be disastrously interpreted or misinterpreted; being the object of public attack; and risking periodic under-employment. We suspect that few of us have among our friends a person whose sober judgement and intelligence we respect, who would consider running for Congress, much less one capable of mounting a respectable campaign. We know of no studies of the psychology of persons choosing political careers but clearly an unusual personality would be needed and some of Hitler's traits, in particular his conviction of the essential rightness of his outlook and his unwavering belief that he had something unique and essential to offer, would be assets and perhaps even essential to anyone choosing such a career. This of course does not mean that today's professional politicians are incipient Hitlers. It does mean that we have created a political environment which encourages highly selected people to make careers in politics and that some of the traits that seem logically strongly selected for are those Hitler also possessed. Unless that environment is altered, there is some danger that in the long perspective of history Hitler may prove to be only the first of his line.

Physical examinations 1923–1945

1923	Mar–Nov	Landsberg prison: Normal physical and psychiatric examination. Fit for trial.
1935	May	Dr Carl von Eicken: Polyp on right vocal cord 1 cm diameter. Tonsils scarred, tympanic membranes normal. 23 May: Polyp removed. Follow-up examinations normal up to 8 August, when acute pharyngitis developed.
1936	20 May	Dr von Eicken: Complaint from Hitler of high metallic ringing in left ear at night. Examination of ears normal.
1936		Dr Theo Morell: Actual extent of examination unknown. Morell implied that it was thorough. Wt 70 kg, Ht 176 cm. Positive findings: (1) swelling in pyloric region; (2) left lobe of liver enlarged; (3) tenderness in area of right kidney; (4) eczema of left leg; (5) scar left thigh; (6) extensive dental repair.
1937		Morell: Eczema of leg disappeared. Tenderness over maxillary and ethmoid sinuses. Blood pressure averaged 143/100 but ranged up to 200 systolic when Hitler excited. Heart rate about 72.
1940	9 Jan	Morell: Blood pressure 140/100, pulse 72.
1942	Autumn	Morell: Tremor observed.
1944	20–23 July	Morell, Giesing, von Hasselbach: Injuries from assassination attempt of 20 July. Contusions right arm and forearm. First degree burns both thighs. Perforations of eardrums bilaterally. 22 July: Temperature 37·.2°,

pulse 82. Whisper heard at 10 cm on left, 5 cm right. Nystagmus to right, falling to right. Reactions of pupils to light and accommodation normal. Eczema of shin, pustules and furuncles back of neck. Deviation of nasal septum to right. August: Infection right ear but drums healed. Tremor greatly lessened or disappeared.

1944	25 Aug	Blood pressure 143/87.
1944	27 Sept	Bronzing of skin, icterus of sclera.
1944	8 Oct	Perforations of eardrums completely closed, infection healed, hearing normal.
1944	25 Nov	Vocal cord polyp, right.
1945		Left patellar reflex increases (Morell).
1945	Feb	Loehlein: Eye examination. Distance vision: Right 3/12, correctable to 5/6 with 1·5 diopter sphere; Left 5/6. Close vision (25–30 cm): Right (+4·0 diopter sph) Nieden II; Left (+3·0 diopter sph) Nieden I. (These results are consistent with 'farsightedness'.) Lid apparatus normal. Mobility normal. Anterior eye normal. Pupils equal, round, normal reactions. Ophthalmoscopic examination after pupils dilated: Left—Retinal vessels normal, media exceptionally clear, papilla normal; Right—'Background was obscured by a delicate veil. Under magnification this appeared as a very delicate, faintly mobile diffuse turbidity of the vitreous humour obviously composed of infinitesimal particles.' Retina not as clearly seen as on left but 'vessels and papilla normal'. Tonometric examination: 'Both eyes 8 with weight of 7·5' (normal).
1945		'Ashcan' doctors report on Hitler. Drs Brandt, Giesing, and von Hasselbach while in American POW camp were asked to fill

out a comprehensive report which included questions usually asked only by medical students. Because there was nothing better to do, the physicians greatly elaborated their responses. All positive findings are described above. In view of the circumstances of the report, there is no reason to list the negative findings but, in fact, none is surprising.

All from Morell

Laboratory, X-ray, Electrocardiography

1936–1944

1936		Blood group A. 'Dysbacterial' flora in intestinal tract.
1940	10–15 Jan	Blood sugar 110 mg per cent, calcium 11·3 mg per cent. Sedimentation rate normal. Wassermann, Meinicke and Kahn normal. Red blood cell count 4·7 million/ml, hemoglobin 97 per cent, white blood cells 5,000/ml. White blood cell differential: basophils 1 per cent, eosinophils 6 per cent, neutrophils 60 per cent, lymphocytes 28 per cent, monocytes 5 per cent.

Urinalysis	11 Jan	21 Dec
Reaction	alkaline	acid
Albumin	negative	fine
Sugar	negative	negative
Urobilinogin	positive	slight increase

1944	Sept	'Increased urobilinogin and urobilin urine dark brown at times.'
1944	19 Sept	Sinus X-rays: shadowing due to infection of maxillary sinuses.
1944	18 Nov	X-ray: maxillary sinuses infected.

ELECTROCARDIOGRAMS

These were redrawn so as to exactly reproduce the original tracing, Dr Karl Weber's reports (translated) are appended.

151

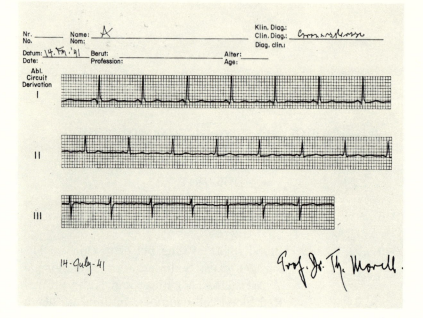

Electrocardiogram I, 14 July 1941   age 51

DIAGNOSIS: Coronary sclerosis

Rate 88   PQRS interval 0·10–11   QRS 0·08

Rhythm: Pacemaker apparently in upper Tarawa node

Lead I: Slight slurring of QR, voltage of T 0·20 mm, slight depression of R–T, slight notching of P, small Q present, R wave 12 mm, P wave 0–0·5 mm.

Lead II: Slight slurring of R, voltage of T (0·5 mm), low take off S–T segment, R-wave 5 mm, P wave 0·3–0·4 mm.

Lead III: Slight slurring of RS, diphasic P, R wave 1·8 mm, S wave 5–6 mm, slight arrhythmia.

Standardization present

Horizontal spacing: 0·04 sec

Vertical spacing: 1 mm

Actual square-spacing: 0·075″

152

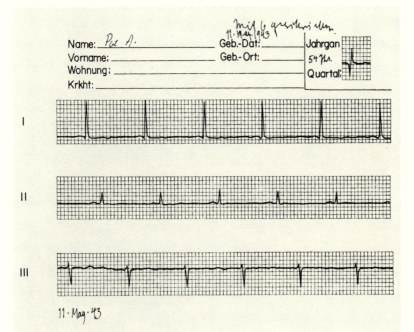

Electrocardiogram II, 11 May 1943   age 54

DIAGNOSIS: Coronary sclerosis

  Rate 85–90   P–QRS interval 0·08

  Rhythm: Pacemaker in upper Tawara node or in lowest sinus
    node

  Axis deviation: Left

  Lead I: Slight notching of base of R, low-inverted T, very
    slight low take off of R–T segment, P-wave 3 mm, R-wave
    9·5 mm, Q-wave 0·75 mm.

  Lead II: Slurring of R, practically isoelectric T, low take off of
    RS–T segment, voltage of P 3 mm, voltage of R 3 mm.

  Lead III: Slight slurring of R–S, low voltage; nearly isoelectric
    T, voltage of R 1 mm, voltage of S 5·5 mm.

  NOTE: Standardization not present

    Horizontal spacing: 0·04 sec

    Vertical spacing: 1 mm

    Actual square-spacing: 0·075″

Electrocardiogram of 4 May 1944
Tracing not in record. Morell describes:
'I and II lead: isoelectric T-strong muscle current'

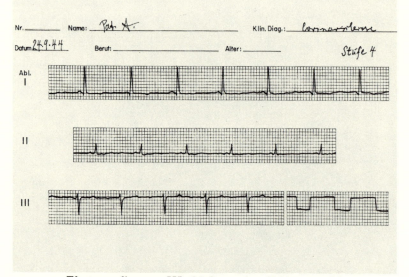

Electrocardiogram III, 24 September 1944   age 55
DIAGNOSIS: Switch on A (sic)
    Rate 85–90   P–QRS interval 0·10–11   QRS 0·08
    Rhythm: Pacemaker apparently in upper Tawara node (con-
        duction time: 0·10–11)
    Axis deviation: Left
    Lead I: Low inverted T, slight low take off of R–T segments,
        notching of P, voltage of P 0·3 mm, small Q-wave (1 mm),
        voltage of R 8·5 mm
    Lead II: Slight slurring of R, isoelectric T, low take off of R–T
        segment, voltage of P 0·3 mm, voltage of R 3 mm
    Lead III: Slight slurring of base of R, voltage of R 1·3 mm,
        voltage of S 5 mm
    NOTE: Standardization present
        Horizontal spacing: 0·04 sec
        Vertical spacing: 1 mm
        Actual square-spacing: 0·075″

154

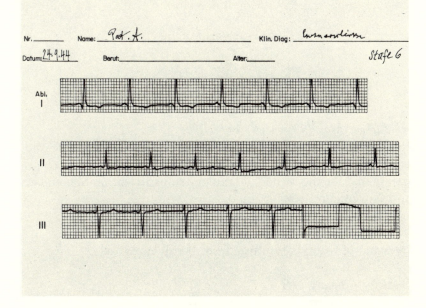

Nr._____ Name: *Pat. A.*_____ Klin. Diag: _____

Datum: 24.9.44 Beruf:_____ Alter:_____ *Stufe 6*

Abl. I

II

III

Electrocardiogram IV 24 September 1944 age 55

DIAGNOSIS: Coronary sclerosis, later, rapidly progressive coronary sclerosis

Rate 85–90   P–QRS interval 0·10–11   QRS 0·08

Rhythm: Pacemaker apparently in upper Tawara node (conduction time 0·10–11)

Axis deviation: Left

Lead I: Notching of P, inverted T, low take off of R–T segment

Lead II: Slight slurring of R, isoelectric T, low take off of R–T segment

Lead III: Very slight slurring of R–S

NOTE: Standardization increased

Horizontal spacing: 0·04 sec

Vertical spacing: 1 mm

Actual square-spacing: 0·075″

155

Treatments 1936–1945

von Eicken: May 1936 and November 1944
Removal of benign polyps from right vocal cord. Morphine and pontocaine anesthesia. Dr Rössle, pathologist, reported 'benign papilloma' for the second. Maxillary sinus irrigation September and November 1944.

von Hasselbach: 20–21 July 1944
Dressing of wounds resulting from bomb explosion.

Loehlein: February 1944
Local heat to eye. Bifocal glasses prescribed

	Right	*Left*
Distant vision	+1·5 diopter	0 diopter
Near vision	+4·0 diopter	3·0 diopter

1 per cent JK solution in right eye daily (1 per cent cocaine).

Giesing: July–October 1944
Repeated cauterization and massage of eardrums. Clearing blood and later pus from eustachian tube. Topical cocaine anesthesia used (10 per cent cocaine).

Morell: 1936—1945
The following is taken directly from the Morell interrogation record. Spelling is as in original:

Medication by Dr Morell
The following is an almost complete list of the drugs used by Dr Morell during his treatment of Hitler. Some were used almost

every day, while others were administered only when the need arose.

Morphia, hypnotics, etc., are not included in this list. But it does contain the names of substances which have a very rapid effect. Glucose, for example, is absorbed quite rapidly and consequently produces a feeling of well-being. Hitler might have dealt with situations very differently after a glucose injection.

Constant medication over a period of years may have upset the physiological balance of his body to such an extent that even normally harmless drugs would be relied on. Thus a person may become dependent on such medication even though the substances employed are not drugs of a habit-forming nature.

(1) ULTRASEPTYL

One tablet of 2-(*p*-aminobenzolsolfonamido)-4-methylthiazol contained 0.5 g. These tablets were prescribed by Dr Morell because Hitler suffered from persistent catarrhal inflamations of the upper respiratory tract and angina. Application: 1–2 tables per os, with addition of much fluid (fruit juice or water) after a meal. Fluid was taken in order to prevent the formation of calculi. Reference: Ultraseptyl-Sanabo, Vienna XII/82.

(2) EUBASIN

A sulfa drug. One ampoule equals 5 cc. Injected intragluteally. Was only injected one, since it caused pain. Therapeutically used for colds.

(3) CHINYEURIN

Hamma product. Prepared by Dr Mulli. This drug contains some chinin. Application per os, after a meal. Therapeutically used against colds. It was used in place of Ultraseptyl.

(4) OMNADIN

Omnadin is a mixture of proteins, lipoid substances of gall and animalic fats, supposed to have all antigenic properties and there-fore· should be used at the beginning of infections. It is nearly specific against colds. Dr Morell preferred Omnadin over

Ultrasepytyl because it was non-toxic. At times Omnadin was given in conjunction with Vitamultin–CA. 1 Ampoula—2 cc was given intramuscularly at a time. Omnadin was used whenever Hitler was afflicted with colds and as a substitute for Ultraseptyl.

(5) PENICILLIN-HAMMA

Prepared by Dr Mulli. Penicillin was used once in form of powder, on a skin wound on Hitler's right hand, 8–10 days after the attempt on his life 20 July 1944. The skin wound was of pea size.

(6) OPTALIDON

A propriatory analgesic, a combination of amidopyrine and barbiturate: containing Sandoptal (a proprietary hypnotic-iso-butylallyl barbituric acid): 0·05: Dimethylamino phenazon (pyramidon): 0·125: Caffein: 0·025. Application: 1–2 tablets per os, was used for headaches.

(7) BROM-NERVACIT

Composed of KBr 4%, NA3PO4 0·1%, Naphodyl 1%; diethyls-barbitur acid phenyldimethylpyrazolon, spiritus, sacch, et sacch t. fact. Aroma. Used as sedative in order to induce sleep and when excited. Dosage: 1–2 tablespoons. In order to prevent a Bromine reaction Dr Morell prescribed it only every other 2 months.

(8) SEPTOIOD

Product of Diwag Chemical factory, AG, Berlin-Waidmannslust. Dr Morell used Septoid against respiratory infections. He also thought it would prevent the progress of Hitler's arteriosclerosis, and used it in place of Ultraseptyl. At times it was applied intravenously up to a maximum dose of 20 cc.

(9) CIRCULATORY ANALEPTICS

CARDIAZOL (Pentamethylentetrazol)
CORAMIN (Pyridin-B-carbonic acid-diethylamid)
In 41, Dr Morell observed edema on external and internal malleoli of fibulae and tibiae; in order to overcome the circulatory

insufficiency and to stimulate circulation, cardiazol and coramin were administered. It was used in the form of a solution of which 10 drops were given internally for the period of a week, after that medication was discontinued for a month, used occasionally again when edema became manifest.

(10) SYMPATHOL

Para-oxyphenylethanolmethylamin, only 1/100 as effective as adrenalin. It was administered by Dr Morell in order to increase the heart-minute-volume of blood. It regulates heart activity and overcomes vessel insufficiency. It was supplied in solution and applied internally, 10 drops a day for temporary periods since 42.

(11) STROPHANTIN

A crystalline glucoside, used as a heart tonic. Electrocardiograms of Hitler suggested coronary sclerosis in 1941. Dr Morell therefore instituted treatment with intravenous injections of strophantin, giving 0·02 mg a day for periods of approximately 2–3 weeks. This type of treatment was repeated several times during the last 3 years.

(12) PROSTROPHANTA

Supplied in ampoules, each containing 0·3 mg of strophantin in combination with glucose and Vitamin B complex (nicotinic acid). Was used same as strophantin.

(13) VITAMULTIN–CA

Contained: A, B, C complex, C, D, E, K, P. It was supplied by Hamma, GMBH, Hamburg, in form of ampoules and tablets. Has been produced since 38. Dr Morell injected 4.4 cc intragluteally every other day. He also prescribed tablets which Hitler sometimes used. It was used from 38 to 44 with short interruptions. It often was taken in combination with other drugs.

(14) INTELAN

Consists of Vitamins A, D, and glucose. Used therapeutically just as Vitamultine, in order to induce appetite, overcome tiredness and strengthen body resistance. Intelan was given in later years, from 42–44. It was supplied in tablet form and was taken twice a day, at meals.

(15) GLUCOSE

Glucose (5–10%) solution was given in order to supply calories. Also used as a mixer with, and to counteract the contractive effect of, strophantin. It was injected intravenously every 2nd or 3rd day (10 cc) for a period of years (from 37–40) with brief interruptions.

(16) TONOPHOSPHAN

Bayer product. It is the sodium salt of dimethyl-amino-methyl-phenyl-phosphinic acid. It is a stimulant for unstriped muscles and was also given to supply phospher. It is supplied in ampoules and tablets. Ampoule contains a 1–2% solution, tablet 0·1 g. Tonophosphan was administered subcutaneously and was used only temporarily during the years 42–44.

(17) MUTAFLOR

It is an emulsion, a particular strain of Bacillus coli communis, and prepared in enteric soluble capsules. Reference: Prof Nissle, Hageda, A. G., Berlin NW 21. Questions regarding the product were directed to Prof Nissle at Freiburg, i B.

According to Prof Nissle, certain strains of Bacillus coli communis have the property of colonizing the intestinal tract. Such a property is not demonstrated by the Yoghurt or acidophylus Bacillus. Because Hitler suffered so much from indigestion (36-40), Dr Morell thought an abnormal bacterial flora of intestinal tract was the cause. A faecal examination proved this was the case. Dr Morell therefore instituted treatment with Mutaflor. It relieved Hitler of some of the pain and of indigestion. As the supply of Mutaflor diminished as a result of the war, former teacher, Prof Laves of University of Graz made a similar Coli preparation, named Trocken Coli Hamma. Prof Laves also examined Hitler's faeces and concluded dysbacterial intestinal flora. Mutaflor treatment consisted of administering a series of capsules: on the first day a yellow capsule, from the 2nd to the 4th day one red capsule per day, and from then on 2 red capsules per day for a period of many years (36–43), with some interruptions. (Trocken Coli Hamma used as substitute).

(18) LUIZYM

This is a digestive enzyme preparation containing ferments which split cellulose, hemicellulose and carbohydrates. It was used for digestive weakness, meteorism, and to make vegetable food more digestible. (Hitler was a vegetarian.)

It was supplied in tablets or dragees. Luizym was taken once in a while when flatus and indigestion became worse. Dose: 1 tablet after meals.

(19) GLYCONORM

Dr Morell treated Hitler with Glyconorm (2 cc injected intramuscularly) in order to check digestive disturbance. It was used only rarely and only during the years 38–40.

It is also supplied in bean form. It is mainly used for the prevention of pellagra. Glyconorm contains metabolic ferments (Cozymase I and II) vitamins, and amino acids.

Produced by NordeMark Werke/Hamburg.

(20) DR KOESTER'S ANTIGAS PILLS

Contains: extr. Nux vom., extr. Bellad. aa0·5, extr. Gent. 1·0—2–4 pills were taken at every meal for a period of many years from 36–43 with temporary interruptions because Hitler suffered from meteorism. Dr Brandt and Dr Giesing think the cumulative effect of this drug produced the icteric discolouration of skin and sclera and epigastric cramps noted Sep 44.

(21) EUFLAT

Combined preparation of radix angelica, papaverin, aloe, active bile extracts, coffee-charcoal, adsorb. pancreas extract. Was supplied in pill form and used orally for better digestion and against meteorism. This drug was only used during years 39–44.

(22) EUKODAL (Dihydro-oxycodeinonchlorhydrate) and
EUPAVERINUM (synthetic alkaloid)
Both were taken for epigastric cramps. Was injected intraven-
ously whenever cramps and pain became manifest.

(24) CAMOMILE
Used frequently for cleansing enemas, which Hitler administered
himself.

(25) PROGYNON
Progynon B. pleosun is an esther of benzoic acid and the dihyd-
rofollicle hormon. It is standardized in international benzoate
units.

 1 ampoule has 1 mg (10·000 I B U). It was given intramuscularly. It increases the circulation of gastric mucesa, and prevents
spasm of gastric wall and vessels. Dr Morell instituted treatment
when Hitler suffered from gastroduodenitis 37–38.

(26) ORCHIKRIN
Is a combination of all hormones of males. Potency is increased by
the addition of extracts of testis, seminal vesicles and prostate of
young bulls. Dr Morell claims to have used it only once and then
in order to combat fatigue and depression. It is administered
intramuscularly 2·2 cc (one ampoule). It is a Hamma product.

(27) PROSTAKRIMUM
An extract of seminal vesicles and prostata. Used to prevent
depressive moods. Was used for a short period in the year 1943.
Dosage: 2 ampoules intramuscularly every second day.

(28) CORTIRON
Desoxycoticosteronacetate. Was injected intramuscularly. Was
used for muscle weakness and to influence the carbohydrate
metabolism and fat resorption. Was used a few times only.

4. *Comments and recommendations*
Further reports on this subject containing additional descriptive

date relating to the physical and mental make-up of Hitler and drawn from sources which were at one time or another in intimate contact with him are contemplated.

The recipients of this report are requested to submit special briefs on any subject on which these sources should be interrogated and to indicate the desirable distribution of resulting reports.

WHG (Gruendl)
H M (Merl)
(Ed: WSM)

For the Commanding Officer:

FRANCIS C ST JOHN
2nd Lt., Infantry
Chief Editor

29 Nov 45
DISTRIBUTION 'D'

Notes and References

Author's Introduction
1. Schramm (1971), pp. 129–33.

CHAPTER ONE   FIRST ILLNESS
1. Speer (1970) p. 104. Speer's description of Hitler's abdominal illness is the most complete with respect to the onset. Morell (1945) confirms the important point that the pain began *after* eating. Krebs (1976) gives medically useful details regarding pain.
2. Speer (1975). In our interview Speer confirmed his written description and added this and a few other minor points.
3. Morell (1945B).
4. Dietrich (1955) p. 142, Schramm (1971) p. 17. Give examples of specific steps taken by Hitler to enhance and improve his image.
5. Von Hasselbach (1975).
6. Von Eicken (1945).
7. Maser (1973) does say that Hitler had a 'complete examination' in January 1940. Maser gives no reference supporting this statement and we find no other mention of it. Hitler did at that time have some blood and urine chemistry done and it appears that this is what Maser refers to. However, those examinations were quite superficial and physicians who knew Hitler are unanimous in saying that he never had the needed complete work up. In particular, he had no X-ray examinations.
8. Dietrich (1955) p. 204 for quote. Krebs (1976) pp. 164–5 describes a conversation with Hitler about vegetarian diet and its relation to his stomach cramps.
9. Speer (1970) p. 65.
10. Fest (1973) p. 535.
11. Speer (1970) p. 106 for quote. This was a very common theme for Hitler mentioned by many observers.
12. Baumbach (1960) pp. 35–9 ff.
13. Morell (1945B) Annex I, Maser (1973) pp. 211.
14. Morell (1936–45) especially microfilm T–253, roll 45.
15. Morell (1936–45) T–253, roll 45, frame no. 1499147.

164

16. Hoffmann (1955) p. 219.
17. Morell (1945B).
18. Speer (1970) p. 105.
19. Morell (1945B).
20. Hitler (1953).
21. Linge (1975).
22. Von Hasselbach (1975). The jaundice itself is extensively documented but not the manner of its discovery. Von Hasselbach told us that Dr Erwin Giesing who happened to be near by saw the jaundice first. Morell was not at first convinced. Giesing (1945A) gave definite dates for the period of jaundice—27 September–2 October 1944.
23. Brandt (1945B), Hoffmann (1955), Giesing (1945A). The timing is not quite clear but both Giesing and Hoffmann imply that the pain became much worse a few days *before* the jaundice appeared. Brandt described increasing pain *during* the period of jaundice.

CHAPTER TWO   NEUROPSYCHIATRIC ILLNESS

1. Speer (1970) p. 239.
2. Halder (1950) p. 57. Speer (1970) and Keitel (1965) also describe the scene.
3. Schramm (1971) p. 117–18.
4. Von Hasselbach (1945), Linge (1975), Wiedemann (1964) pp. 118 ff.
5. Speer (1970) p. 97.
6. Schellenburg (1956) p. 319. Schellenburg was chief of intelligence on the Eastern Front.
7. Keitel (1965) pp. 182–3.
8. Hoffmann (1955) pp. 208 and 216.
9. Guderian (1952) p. 414.
10. Dietrich (1955) pp. 212 ff.
11. Linge (1975) described the periodicity in some detail. Also, Speer (1970, 1975) gives medically useable data.
12. Assmann (1953).
13. Guderian (1952) p. 442.
14. Kersten (1957).
15. Kesselring (1953) p. 180.
16. Von Rundstedt (1945). The source of both quotations. Von Rundstedt dates the change as 'after 1944' but because he had just returned to headquarters after a long absence, his dating does not help.
17. Ibid.
18. Speer (1970) p. 293.

19. Assmann (1953) makes this point. It is also evident in verbatim transcripts of military conferences published by Gilbert (1950).
20. Dietrich (1955) p. 145.
21. Speer (1970) p. 293.
22. Keitel (1965) p. 146–7.
23. Speer (1970) p. 359.
24. Speer (1975). We clarified the nature of the pathology with Dr Speer.
25. Giesing (1945A).
26. Guderian (1952) p. 342.
27. Dietrich (1955) p. 91.
28. Pihl (1944) p. 93, quotes Morell's diagnosis. We find no other source for this statement—Morell mentions depression only—but Pihl, a Swedish journalist, seems accurate. Speer (1970) p. 294 footnote records Morell's advice which Hitler, of course, did not accept. Morell (1945B), included in Appendix C, describes the treatments for depression.
29. Speer (1970) p. 292.
30. Gilbert (1950) p. 106.
31. Speer (1970) p. 455.
32. Gilbert (1950) pp. 80–2.
33. Schramm (1971) pp. 156 ff.
34. Kesselring (1953) p. 239.
35. Speer (1975).
36. Schenck (1975).
37. Guderian (1952) pp. 342 ff.
38. Dietrich (1955) p. 213.
39. Recktenwald (1958) for example.
40. Deutsche Wochenschau (1945).
41. Guderian (1952) pp. 443 ff., Zoller (1948). Zoller wrote a sensationalized account based on information given him by Krista Schroeder, one of Hitler's secretaries. He describes Hitler as being unable to lie down without help—someone had to pick up his legs and place them on a couch or bed. Generally the source is untrustworthy but this description of Hitler has a ring of truth.
42. Deutsche Wochenschau (1945). However, von Hasselbach and others have commented on Hitler's lack of facial expression. Von Hasselbach told us that he regards Hitler as bordering on the 'masked facies' commonly seen in Parkinsonism. Thus, it may be that Hitler did intermittently exhibit Parkinsonian features as will be discussed in Chapter Seven.
43. Von Hasselbach (1975).
44. Baumbach (1960) p. 148.
45. Guderian (1952) p. 342.

46. Giesing (1945A).
47. Speer (1975).
48. Gebhard (1945) remarked that Hitler was vivacious, rested and seemed perfectly well at this time. Dr Weber (1975) described him as mentally 'normal' (Weber, 1975).
49. Gilbert (1950) pp. 158–74.

CHAPTER THREE   OTHER ILLNESSES
1. Makkus (1975).
2. Makkus (1975) (1976).
3. Morell (1936–45) T–253, roll 35, frame 1486197–9.
4. Linge (1977) told us that he knew of only a few cardiograms. Makkus (1977) told us that Linge was usually away. Makkus was responsible for moving and setting up the cardiograph machine. Sometimes cardiograms wanted by Morell or Hitler were not done because moving and setting up the apparatus would attract too much attention.
5. Von Eicken (1945).
6. Hitler (1925) p. 202.
7. US Army Medical Department (1926) pp. 262 ff.
8. Fest (1973) notes 60 and 63, p. 772. As Fest describes, the military medical records have been lost but personnel documents give the diagnosis which is likely correct.
9. Morell (1945B).
10. Giesing (1945A).
11. Loehlein report in Appendix A.

CHAPTER FOUR   PERSONAL MEDICAL HISTORY
1. Maser (1974) pp. 12–15.
2. Authorities disagree. Maser (1974) Chapter 1, extensively discussed the evidence before concluding that Nepomuk was the father. Toland (1976) is less certain.
3. Fest (1973) p. 20.
4. Hitler (1925) p. 4.
5. Garland (1974).
6. Cf. Smith (1967). This is a useful and authoritative account of Adolf Hitler's early years.
7. Fieve *et al.* (1974) for genetic study of antisocial personality.
8. Toland (1976) p. 17 gives good description.
9. Kubizek (1955).
10. Hitler (1925) pp. 17 and 20.
11. Jetzinger (1958) quoted by Fest (1974) p. 30.
12. Maser (1974) Chapter 3 for review.

13. Toland (1976) pp. 49–51.
14. Speer (1970) p. 101.

CHAPTER FIVE   MEDICAL TREATMENT
1. Gehes Codex (1938) lists the ingredients in Dr Koester's pills. Goodman and Gilman (1972) for data supporting the calculations of dosages.
2. Röhrs (1966), Linge (1975), both said Hitler might rarely have taken as many as twenty pills but that 8–10 daily was more usual.
3. Goodman and Gilman (1972).
4. Linge (1975). Linge does not know just when Hitler started this practice but is sure that it antedated his assumption of power in 1933.
5. Speer (1970) p. 301.
6. Linge (1975). The Morell microfilms also describe the occasional use of leeches on other patients but there is no apparent common denominator within the patient groups.
7. Franck (1934). This book is much like the *Merck Manual* familiar to US physicians. Makkus (1975) told us that this is the only medical book Morell had available.
8. Gehes Codex (1938).
9. Weber (1975).
10. Morell (1936–45) T253–35, frame 1485539, and T253–40, frame 1492393–407.
11. Röhrs (1966) and Fikentscher (1974) have dealt extensively with Morell's erroneous claims about Russlapuder and penicillin.
12. Morell (1936–45) T253–35, frame 1487180. We did not find descriptions of the treatment Mussolini received.
13. Brandt (1945B), Hoffman (1955) p. 120, Speer (1970) p. 105.
14. Linge (1943–5). There is a discrepancy here. Linge's appointment books survive in fragments. From 11 August–30 December 1943 Morell is recorded as visiting in the morning once or twice a week only, although he did see Hitler at other times nearly every day. From 14 October 1944–28 February 1945 Morell does visit nearly every morning. Linge told us that Hitler got injections all through the Russian war which became daily some time during the winter of 1941–2. We think Linge's oral testimony is the most accurate record.
15. Linge (1975).
16. Bezymenski (1968) p. 11.
17. Kersten (1957), Brandt (1945B). Also Kersten quotes Himmler as saying 'after one of Morell's injections Hitler is astonishingly clear

and logical, his thoughts are original as ever they were in the old days'.

18. Junge (1977), Assmann (1953).
19. Schenck (1970) pp. 156–157.
20. Makkus (1978).
21. Linge (1975).
22. Röhrs (1966). Dr Schenck repeated the same story to us.
23. Schenck (1970).
24. Morell (1939–45), 235–43, frames 1497036–39 and 1497085.
25. Morell (1939–45), 235–43, frame 1496861–63.
26. Jost (1975), Hildegard Jost, who worked in a Berlin pharmacy through the war and was married to a pharmacist who worked at the Engel Apotheke, told us that at the practical day-to-day operational level Göring had great difficulty obtaining illicit drugs and Morell would have had the same problems to obtain a regulated drug even for Hitler.
27. Morell (1936–45). Cf. roll T–253 No. 45, frame 1499197, letter from Engel Apotheke to Morell, 29 August 1942.
28. Giesing (1945A).
29. Makkus (1978).
30. Morell (1936–45) T–253-35, frame 1485985.
31. Morell (1936–45) T–253-35, frame 1485984.
32. Morell (1936–45) T–253-43. frame 1497011.
33. Morell (1936–45) T–253-43, frame 1495727.
34. Morell (1936–45) T–253-43, frame 1495706.
35. Morell (1936–45) T–253-34, frames 1485334 and 1490565.
36. Giesing (1945A).
37. Woolverton and Schuster (1978).
38. Fischman *et al.* (1976).
39. Inquiries were sent or personally taken to the National Archives; Imperial War Museum; Bundesarchiv; Ministrere de la Défense, Service Historique; Archives de France; and the Defense Intelligence Agency citing the Freedom of Information Act.
40. Morell (1945 A and B).
41. Morell (1936–45) T–253-35, frames 148533–54 and 14853510–37.
42. Von Hasselbach (1975).

CHAPTER SIX   AMPHETAMINE

1. Kalant (1966). The source of the quotation and an excellent general review of the clinical pharmacology. Also Ellinwood and Cohen (1972) for more basic pharmacology and Bett *et al.* (1955), Jackson (1975) for history and clinical features.
2. Halpern and Citron (1971), Margolis and Newton (1971).
3. Patel (1972).

CHAPTER SEVEN DIAGNOSES

1. Bezymenski (1968).
2. Sognases and Ström, F. (1973).
3. Bezymenski (1968) pp. 68–9.
4. Speer (1975).
5. Speer (1975, 1976). Dr Speer described the biting to us and mentioned it briefly in his book, p. 236. Linge (1975) independently confirmed Dr Speer and said that he was sure there was occasional biting as early as 1938.
6. Linge (1975).
7. Linge (1975). Linge stated that the scratching seemed to replace the biting in some way. The more Hitler scratched, the less he bit.
8. Junge (1977).
9. Linge (1977).
10. Wykes (1970) for example, offers the diagnosis but presents extremely weak evidence, pp. 14–17 Kersten (1957) p. 165, quotes Himmler's diagnostic opinion.
11. The experts were Drs Irving I. Gottesman, Leonard L. Heston, and Paul E. Meehl. The author feels that offering an estimate himself is justified in these special circumstances. For further reading into this difficult area see Gottesman and Shields (1972), Heston (1970), Meehl (1962) (1970).
12. Janowsky *et al.* (1973).
13. Waite (1977).
14. Binion (1973) for this theory and many additional examples of what should be quickly forgotten.
15. Toland (1976) xviii–xix.
16. Waite (1977) p. 424, note.
17. Walshe (1940) quoted by L'Etang (1974).

CHAPTER EIGHT HITLER MEDICINE AND HISTORY

1. Irving (1977) p. 294.
2. Henderson (1940) p. 108.
3. Speer (1970) p. 84.
4. Kersten (1957) p. 165.
5. Ciano (1953) p. 113.
6. Linge (1977).
7. Cf. Toland (1976) pp. 515–17 for examples.
8. Hoffmann (1955) p. 94.
9. Toland (1976) pp. 517–20, Taylor (1964) pp. 250–4, discuss the dramatic change in world opinion.
10. Keitel (1965) pp. 161–4. Also Halder (1950) p. 52 describes Hitler's impulsivity and temper during this period.
11. Keitel (1965) pp. 167–8.

12. Irving (1977).
13. Jäckel (1972).
14. Speer (1970) pp. 362–5, discusses the development of jet aircraft and rockets.
15. Speer (1970) p. 295.
16. Morell (1936–45) roll 37, frame 1488404–05.
17. Morell (1936–45) roll 37, frame 1488397.
18. Linge (1977).
19. Linge (1945).
20. Irving (1977) p. 799, states the eyedrops contained cocaine but does not give a source. However, he is almost certainly correct because we cannot imagine any other reason for the increased dosage. 'JK' could well stand for Jod-Kokain (iodine-cocaine) which was a very common preparation containing 1 per cent cocaine which Morell ordered often from the Engel Apotheke.

Afterword
1. L'Etang (1969).
2. Thomas (1967) p. 100.
3. Bishop (1977).
4. Alliluyeva (1967).
5. Wilson (1966). Churchill took several pills which he named 'greens', 'reds, Moran specials' and so on. The information is scattered through the book but nearly all of it is indexed under 'Churchill; medications'.
6. Speer (1970) pp. 519–26.

Appendices
1. All data come from the following sources: Landsberg prison 'Hausärztlicher Ambulanten-Rapport' (1923), von Eicken (1945), Morell (1945B), Giesing (1945 A and B), von Hasselbach (1945), Loehlein (1945).

References

Alliluyeva, S. (1967) *Twenty Letters to a Friend*, P. J. McMillan, trans., New York, Harper and Row [Priscilla Johnson, trans., London, Hutchinson].

Assmann, H. (1953) 'Some recollections of Adolf Hitler', R. E. Krause, trans., US Naval Inst. Proceedings 79, 1289–95.

Baumbach, W. (1960) *The Life and Death of the Luftwaffe*, F. Holt, trans., NY, Coward-McCann [*Broken Swastika—The defeat of the Luftwaffe*, London, Robert Hale].

Bett, W. R., Howells, L. H., and MacDonald, A. D. (1955) *Amphetamine in Clinical Medicine: Actions and Uses*, Edinburgh, E. and S. Livingstone Ltd.

Bezymenski, L. (1968) *The Death of Adolf Hitler: Unknown Documents from Soviet Archives*, NY, Harcourt, Brace and World Inc. [London, Michael Joseph].

Binion, Rudolph (1973) 'Hitler's concept of *Lebensraum*: The psychological basis'. *History of Childhood Quarterly*, Fall 1973, pp. 187–258.

Bishop, J. (1974) *FDR's Last Year: April 1944—April 1945*, NY, William Morrow and Company, Inc. [London, Rupert Hart-Davis, 1975].

Brandt, K. (1945A) *Hitler as seen by his doctors*. Consolidated interrogation report (CIR) No. 2, 01–CIR/2, 15 Oct 1945, Modern Military Records Division, National Archives, Washington, DC.

Brandt, K. (1945B) *Dr Karl Brandt: His career, his position as Reich Commissioner for Health and Medical Services, Medical Information, Notes on Dr. Morell*. CCPWE 32/DI–17, 30 June 1945, Modern Military Records Division, National Archives, Washington, DC.

Ciano, G. (1953) *Ciano's Hidden Diary 1937–1938*, A. Mayor, trans., NY, E. P. Dutton [*Ciano's Diary 1937–1938*, London, Methuen and Co., 1952].

Deutsche Wochenschau (1945) German newsreel excerpts. 242 .210- .311, National Archives Audiovisual Division, National Archives, Washington, DC.

Dietrich, O. (1955) *Hitler*, R. and C. Winston, trans., Chicago, Henry Regnery Co. (London, Methuen and Co., 1957).

Eicken, C. von (1945) Notes of Professor von Eicken, Modern Military Records Division, National Archives, Washington, DC.

References

Ellinwood, E. H., and Cohen, S., Eds. (1972) *Current concepts on amphetamine abuse*, Department of Health, Education and Welfare Publication no. (HSM) 72–9085, USGPO, Washington, DC.

Fest, J. C. (1973) *Hitler*, R. and C. Winston, trans., NY, Harcourt Bruce Javanovich, Inc. [London, Weidenfeld and Nicolson, 1974].

Fieve, R. R., Rosenthal, D., and Brill, H., Eds. (1975) *Genetic Research in Psychiatry*, Part I: Genetic studies of criminology and psychopathy, Baltimore, John Hopkins University Press.

Fikentscher, H. (1972) 'Hitler's Leibarzt Morell', *Zetung für historische Wahrheitsforschung*, 1, 17–24.

Fischman, M. W., Schuster, C. R., Resnekow, L., Shick, J. F. E., Krasnegor, N. A., Fennell, W., and Freedman, D. X. (1976) 'Cardiovascular and subjective effects of intravenous cocaine administration in humans', *Arch. Gen. Psychiat.*, 33, 983–9.

Franck, R. (1934) *Moderne Therapie*, Berlin, Springer-Verlag.

Garland, R. (1974) Personal communication.

Gebhardt, K. F. (1945) Interrogation, Bundesarchiv.

Gehes Codex (1938) München, Schwarzeck-Verlag GMBH.

Giesing, E., (1945A) Deposition, Bundesarchiv.

Giesing, E. (1945B) Preliminary Interrogation Report (PIR) 4 June 1945, and Hitler as seen by his doctors, Consolidated Interrogation Report (CIR) 15 October 1945, Modern Military Records Division, National Archives, Washington, DC.

Gilbert, F. (1950) *Hitler Directs His War: The Secret Records of His Daily Military Conferences*, New York, Oxford.

Goodman, L. S., and Gilman, A. (1972) *The Pharmacological Basis of Therapeutics*, 4th ed., NY, Macmillan.

Gottesman, I. I., and Shields, J. (1972) *Schizophrenia and Genetics: a twin study vantage point*, NY, Academic Press.

Guderian, H. (1952) *Panzer Leader*, C. Fitzgibbon, trans., London, M. Joseph.

Halder, F. (1950) *Hitler as War Lord*, London, Putnam.

Halpern, M., and Citron, B. P. (1971) 'Necrotizing angitis associated with drug abuse', *Amer. J. Roentgen*, 111, 663–71.

Hasselbach, H. K. von (1945) *Hitler as seen by his doctors*, 01–CIR-2, 15 Oct 1945, Modern Military Records Division, National Archives, Washington, DC.

Hasselbach, H. K. von (1975) Interview.

Henderson, N. (1940) *Failure of a Mission: Berlin 1937–1939*, NY, Putnam [London, Hodder and Stoughton].

Heston, L. L. (1970) 'The Genetics of Schizophrenic and Schizoid Disease', *Science*, 167, 249–56.

Hitler, A. (1925) *Mein Kampf*, R. Manheim, trans., Sentry edition,

Houghton Mifflin, Boston, 1943 [London, Hurst and Blackett, 1939, trans., James Murphy].

Hitler, A. (1953) *Hitler's secret conversations: 1941-1944*, N. Cameron and R. H. Stevens, trans., NY, Farrar Straus and Young, Inc. [London, Weidenfeld and Nicolson, *Hitler's Table Talk 1941–1944*].

Hoffmann, H. (1955) *Hitler Was My Friend*, R. H. Stevens, trans., London, Burke.

Irving, D. (1977) *Hitler's War*, NY, Viking Press (London, Hodder and Stoughton).

Jackson, C. O. (1975) 'The amphetamine democracy: medicinal abuse in the popular culture', *So. Atlantic Quarterly*, **74**, 308–23.

Jäckel, E. (1972) *Hitler's Weltanschauung: a blueprint for power*, H. Arnold, trans., Middletown, Conn., Wesleyan Univ. Press.

Janowsky, D. S., El-Yousef, K. L., Davis, J. M., and Sekerke, H. J. (1973) 'Provocation of schizophrenic symptoms by intravenous administration of methylphenidate', *Arch. Gen. Psychiat.*, **28**, 185–91.

Jetzinger, F. (1958) *Hitler's Youth*, London, Hutchinson.

Jost, H. (1975) Interview.

Junge, T. (1977) Interview.

Kalant, O. J. (1966) *The Amphetamines: Toxicity and Addiction*, Springfield, C. C. Thomas.

Keitel, W. (1965) *The Memoirs of Field-Marshal Keitel*, Walter Gorlitz, Ed., D. Irving, trans., London, William Kimber (New York, Stein and Day).

Kersten, F. (1957) *The Kersten Memoirs 1940–1945*, C. Fitzgibbon and J. Oliver, trans., NY, Macmillan (London, Hutchinson and Co., 1956).

Kesselring, A. (1953) *The Memoirs of Field-Marshal Kesselring*, William Kimber, London.

Krebs, A. (1976) *The Infancy of Nazism*, W. S. Allen, Ed. and trans., NY, New Viewpoints.

Kubizek, A. (1955) *The Young Hitler I Knew*, E. V. Anderson, trans., Boston, Houghton Mifflin Co. [*Young Hitler, The Story of our Friendship*, Allan Wingate, 1954].

Landsberg prison document (1923) Modern Military Records Division, National Archives, Washington, DC.

L'Etang, H. 1969) *The Pathology of Leadership*, London, Heinemann.

L'Etang, H. (1974) 'Psychiatric illness and future of nations', *Proc. Roy. Soc. Med.*, **67**, 619–21.

Linge, H. (1943–45) Microfilm rolls T84–22 and T84–387, National Archives and Records Service, Washington, DC.

Linge, H. (1945) Hitler's appointment pad, 15–28 April 1945, Imperial War Museum, London.

Linge, H. (1975) Interview.

Linge, H. (1977) Interview.

Loehlein, W. (1945) Hitler as seen by his doctors, 01/CIR/4, 29 Nov 1945, Annex III, Modern Military Records Division, National Archives, Washington, DC.

Makkus, R. (1975) Interviews and letters to authors.

Makkus, R. (1976) Interviews and letters to authors.

Makkus, R. (1978) Interviews and letters to authors.

Margolis, M. T., and Newton, T. H. (1971) 'Methamphetamine ("speed") arteritis', *Neuroradiol.*, **2**, 179-86.

Maser, W. (1974) *Hitler: Legend, Myth and Reality*, P. and B. Ross, trans., NY, Harper Row.

Meehl, P. E. (1962) 'Schizotaxia, schizotypy, schizophrenia', *American Psychologist*, **17**, 827–38.

Meehl, P. E. (1972) A critical afterword, in, *Schizophrenia and Genetics: a twin study vantage point*, (by I. I. Gottesman and J. Shields) pp. 367–416, NY, Academic Press.

Morell, T. (1936–45) Microfilmed records, T253, rolls 34–45, National Archives, Washington, DC.

Morell, T. (1945A) Preliminary Interrogation Report 01–PIR 9, 14 Sept 1945, Modern Military Records Division, National Archives, Washington DC.

Morell, T. (1945B) 'Hitler as seen by his doctors', 01/CIR/4, 8 Nov 1945, Modern Military Records Division, National Archives, Washington, DC.

Patel, A. N. (1972) 'Self inflicted strokes', *Ann. Intern. Med.*, **76**, 823–4.

Pihl, G. T. (1944) *Germany: The Last Phase*, G. H. Smith, trans., NY, Alfred A. Knopf.

Recktenwald, J. (1963) *Woran hat Adolf Hitler gelitten: Eine neuropsychiatrische Deutung*, München/Basel, Ernst Reinhardt Verlag.

Röhrs, H. D. (1966) *Hitler's Krankheit: Tatsache und Legende*, Neckergemünde, Kurt Vowenckel Verlag.

Rundstedt, G. von (1945) Interrogation, in Bundesarchiv, Koblenz.

Schellenberg, W. (1956) *Hitler's Secret Service*, L. Hagen, trans., NY, Pyramid Books (London, Andre Deutsch).

Schenck, E. G. (1970) *Ich Sah Berlin Sterben: Als Arzt in Der Reichkanzlei*, Herford, Nicolaische Verlagsbuchhandlung.

Schenck, E. G. (1975) Interview.

Schramm, P. E. (1971) *Hitler: The Man and the Military Leader*, D. S. Detwiler, trans., Chicago, Quadrangle Books (London, Allan Lane, 1972).

Smith, B. F. (1967) *Adolf Hitler: His family, childhood and youth*, Stanford, Cal., The Hoover Institute on war, revolution and peace, Stanford University.

Sognases, R. F., and Ström, F. (1973) 'The odontological identification of Adolf Hitler: definitive documentation by x-rays, interrogations and autopsy findings', *Acta Odontl. Scand.*, **31**, 43–69.

Speer, A. (1970) *Inside the Third Reich*, R. and C. Winston, trans., NY, Macmillan (London, Weidenfeld and Nicolson).

Speer, A. (1975) Interview.

Speer, A. (1976) *Spandau: The Secret Diaries*, R. and C. Winston, trans., NY, Macmillan (London, Wm. Collins and Sons).

Taylor, A. P. J. (1964) *The Origins of the Second World War*, Harmondsworth, Penguin Books.

Thomas, H. (1967) *The Suez Affair*, London, Weidenfeld and Nicholson.

Toland, J. (1976) *Adolf Hitler*, NY, Doubleday.

U.S. Army Medical Dept. (1926) The medical department of the United States Army in the World War, Vol. XIV, *Medical aspects of gas warfare*, Washington, Government printing office.

Waite, R. G. (1977) *The Psychopathic God: Adolf Hitler*, NY, Basic Books.

Walshe, F. (1940) Letter, *Lancet*, **1**, 194.

Weber, R. (1975) Interview.

Wiedemann, F. (1964) *Der Mann, der Feldherr werden wollte*, Velbert.

Wilson, C. (Lord Moran) (1966) *Churchill: taken from the diaries of Lord Moran*, Boston, Houghton-Mifflin Co. [*Winston Churchill: The Struggle for Survival 1940—1965*, London, Constable and Co.].

Woolverton, W. L., and Schuster, C. R. (1978) Behavioral Tolerance to Cocaine, in *Behavioral Tolerance: Research and Treatment Implications*, N. A. Krasnegor, Ed., NIDA Research Monograph 18, US Government Printing Office, Washington, DC.

Wykes, A. (1970) *Hitler*, Ballatine War Leader Book no. 3, NY, Ballantine Books Inc.

Zoller, A. (1949) *Douze ans auprès d'Hitler. Confidences d'une secrétaire particulière d'Hitler*. Paris: Éditions René Julliard.

Index

Göring, Hermann; addiction to morphine, 89; Doctors' quarrel and, 17; Stalingrad air lift promised, 134; teases Morell, 85

Gottesman, Dr Irving I., 23, 170

Great Britain, reaction to Hacha episode, 129

Guderian, General Heinz, anger, Hitler's described, 40; gait, Hitler's described, 51; suspiciousness, Hitler's described, 45

Gypsies, extermination of, 133–134

Hacha, Emil (President of Czechoslovakia): Berlin meeting with Hitler, 127–128; medical records of, 94; physical collapse of, 127–128; treatment of by Morell, 128–129

Halder, Colonel-General, Franz, 39

Hamma (Morell's pharmaceutical co.), 77, 88-89

Harris, Dr John, 23

Hase, Dr, 17

Hasselbach, Dr Hans-Karl von: doctor's quarrel and, 89–91; examinations of Hitler, 52, 148; Morell's treatments, opinions of, 17; Parkinson's disease as Hitler's diagnosis, 122; post war fate, 96; treatment of Hitler, 156; as US prisoner, 96

Hausman, Dr William, 24

Headaches, Hitler's, 22, 59

Heart disease, Hitler's, 56–58

Henderson, Sir Neville, British Ambassador in Berlin, 126

Hepatitis as possible diagnosis for Hitler, 107–108

Heston,. Dr Alan, 23

Hewel, Walter, Foreign Ministry Liaison to Hitler, 83

Himmler, Heinrich: SS leader, change in Hitler in 1938, 127; Hitler's, 'sick mind', 42; Morell's injections, effect of, 83; suppression of report, 86; syphilis as possible diagnosis for Hitler, 115

Hitler, Adolf:
adolescence of, 66–67;
Ardennes offensive and, 48, 49;
attitudes of: antisemitism, 19, 71, 120; toward authority, 30; his image, 30, 31; toward leadership, 42; toward medicine, 30
autopsy of, 111–113
behaviour of: anger, 39, 40–42; change of, 12, 126–129; in diplomatic meetings, 129; impulsiveness, 41; in military meetings, 38, 44, 47; self control of, 40
blood sugar of, 151
boyhood of, 63–67
cardiovascular illness of, 56–59, 123; amphetamine and, 123, 137–138; angina pectoris possible, 137–138; blood pressure, 58; electrocardiograms, 56–57, 151–155; heart failure absent, 58; secrecy maintained, 57–58; treatment attempted, 79–81
concentration camps and, 19
death camps and, 133–134
decorations in World War I, 69
diagnoses listed, 124
ear, nose and throat of, 148–149; 151
eyes of, 60, 61, 115, 124, 142, 149, 156
family of, 63–65
'final solution' and, 133–34
gastrointestinal illness of,